# BEST
# EDITORIAL
# CARTOONS
## OF THE YEAR

ROY PETERSON
Courtesy Vancouver Sun

# BEST EDITORIAL CARTOONS OF THE YEAR

## 2008 EDITION

Edited by
## CHARLES BROOKS

**PELICAN PUBLISHING COMPANY**
GRETNA 2008

**Library of Congress Serial Catalog Data**

Best Editorial Cartoons, 1972-
Gretna [La.] Pelican Pub. Co.
v. 36 cm annual—
"A pictorial history of the year."

United States—Politics and Government—
1969—Caricatures and cartoons—Periodicals.
E839.5B45  320.9'7309240207  73-643645
ISSN 0091-2220                    MARC-S

Printed in the United States of America

Published by Pelican Publishing Company, Inc.
1000 Burmaster Street, Gretna, Louisiana 70053

# Contents

# Award-Winning Cartoons

## 2007 PULITZER PRIZE

## WALT HANDELSMAN

Editorial Cartoonist
*Newsday*

Graduate of the University of Cincinnati; editorial cartoonist for a chain of suburban Baltimore newspapers, 1982-85, the *Scranton Times*, 1985-89, the *New Orleans Times-Picayune*, 1989-2001, and *Newsday*, 2001 to the present; previous winner of the Pulitzer Prize for editorial cartooning; two-time winner of the National Headliner Award; past winner of the Sigma Delta Chi Award and the Scripps-Howard National Journalism Award; creates animated editorial cartoons for *Newsday* seen on the internet; cartoons syndicated by Tribune Media Services.

## MIKE LUCKOVICH

Editorial Cartoonist
*Atlanta Journal-Constitution*

Born January 28, 1960; editorial cartoonist for the *Greenville News*, 1984-85, the *New Orleans Times-Picayune*, 1985-89, and the *Atlanta Journal-Constitution*, 1989 to the present; previous winner of the National Headliner Award for editorial cartooning; past winner of the Pulitzer Prize and the Overseas Press Club Award (twice); cartoons syndicated in 150 newspapers.

# 2006 SIGMA DELTA CHI AWARD
### (Awarded in 2007)

## MIKE LESTER

Editorial Cartoonist
*Rome News-Tribune (Ga.)*

Born March 3, 1955, in Atlanta, Georgia; creator of "Mike du Jour," a daily animated cartoon for Dow.Jones.com; author of several children's books; commercial illustrator for advertising campaigns; cartoons syndicated by Cagle Cartoons.

# 2007 FISCHETTI AWARD

## MIKE KEEFE

Editorial Cartoonist
*The Denver Post*

Born in Santa Rosa, California, in 1946; earned two degrees and completed coursework for Ph.D. in mathematics at the University of Missouri at Kansas City; editorial cartoonist for the *Denver Post* since 1975; previous winner of the Fischetti Award for editorial cartooning, as well as the National Headliner Award and the Sigma Delta Chi Award; past president of the Association of American Editorial Cartoonists.

# 2007 HERBLOCK AWARD

## JIM MORIN

Editorial Cartoonist
*The Miami Herald*

Born January 30, 1953, in Washington, D.C.; editorial cartoonist for the *Miami Herald* since 1978; past winner of the Pulitzer Prize for editorial cartooning and the National Cartoonist Society Editorial Cartoon Award.

# BEST
# EDITORIAL
# CARTOONS
# OF THE YEAR

JIM SIERGEY
Courtesy www.jimsiergey.com

# The Presidential Campaign

The 2008 presidential campaign got off to an early start with Democrat rising star Barack Obama forcing Sen. Hillary Clinton to declare her candidacy earlier than she had planned. The Illinois senator, expected to vie with Clinton for the African-American vote in the 2008 primaries, accused her of flip-flopping on the Iraq war.

New York City Mayor Michael Bloomberg, super-wealthy and capable of financing his own campaign, dropped hints that he might run as an independent. A $400 haircut seemed to have crippled the campaign of former Sen. John Edwards, the early candidate of the far left. Former Vice-president Al Gore, buoyed by winning the Nobel Prize, waited in the wings.

Rudy Giuliani led the early Republican charge, although many felt his stands favoring abortion and gay rights could handicap his candidacy. Actor and former Sen. Fred Thompson added his name to the Republican list in September. Sen. John McCain, a staunch advocate of the war in Iraq, saw early peaks and valleys in his campaign. Former Massachusetts Gov. Mitt Romney won the early Iowa straw poll and sought to dispel suggestions that somehow his Mormon faith should bar him from the Oval Office.

Each party tried to stir interest in the early campaigning by holding a series of televised "debates" among their major candidates.

MIKE THOMPSON
Courtesy Detroit Free Press

JIMMY MARGULIES
Courtesy King Features

RICK KOLLINGER
Courtesy Star Democrat (Md.)

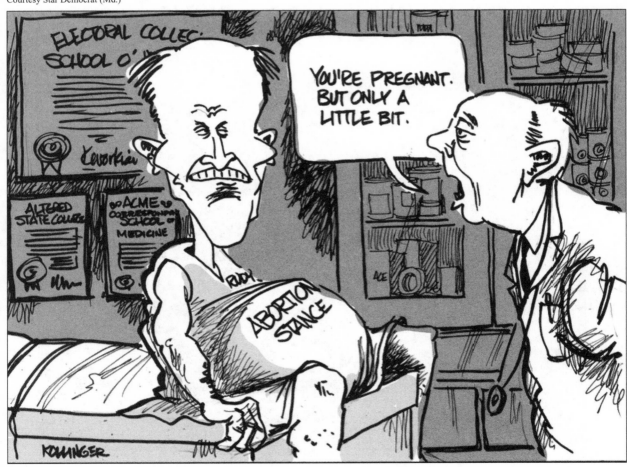

TONY BAYER
Courtesy The News-Dispatch (Ind.)

"I wanted to announce for president, but I can't get on Letterman."

GENE HERNDON
Courtesy Noblesville Daily Times (Ind.)

JOHN R. ROSE
Courtesy Byrd Newspapers/
   Daily News Record (Va.)

PAUL CONRAD
Courtesy Tribune Media Services

BILL SMITH
Courtesy Lompoc Record (Calif.)

WALT HANDELSMAN
Courtesy Newsday

18

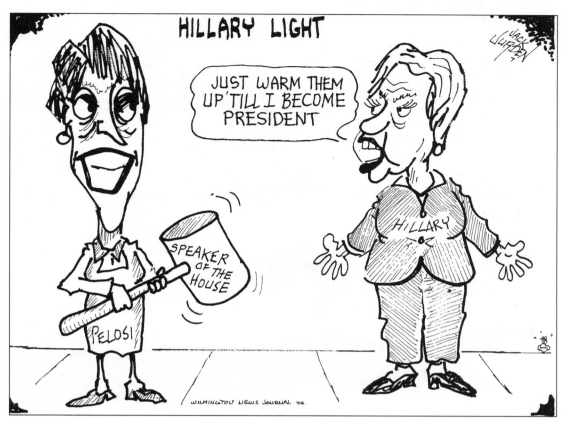

JACK JURDEN
Courtesy Wilmington News Journal

JACK HIGGINS
Courtesy Chicago Sun-Times

STEVE BREEN
Courtesy San Diego Union-Tribune

JOHN BRANCH
Courtesy San Antonio Express-News

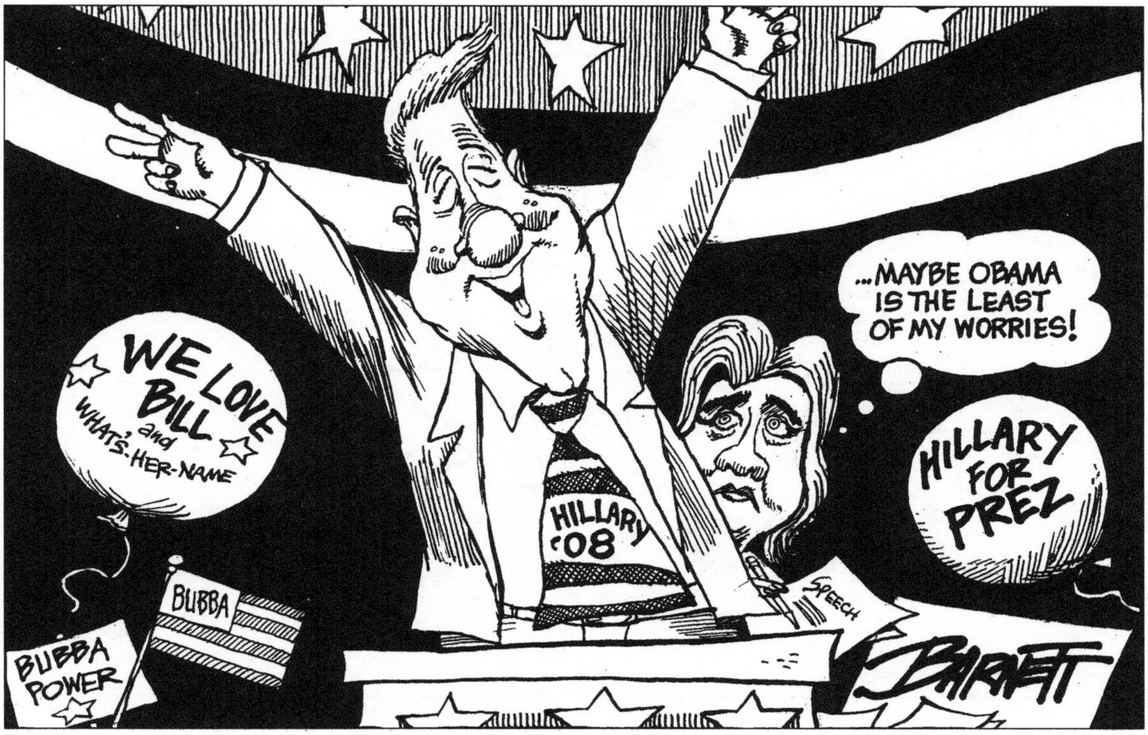
...MAYBE OBAMA IS THE LEAST OF MY WORRIES!
WE LOVE BILL and WHAT'S-HER-NAME
HILLARY '08
HILLARY FOR PREZ
BUBBA
BUBBA POWER
SPEECH
BARNETT

JERRY BARNETT
Courtesy Boonville Standard (Ind.)

GARY MARKSTEIN
Courtesy Copley News Service

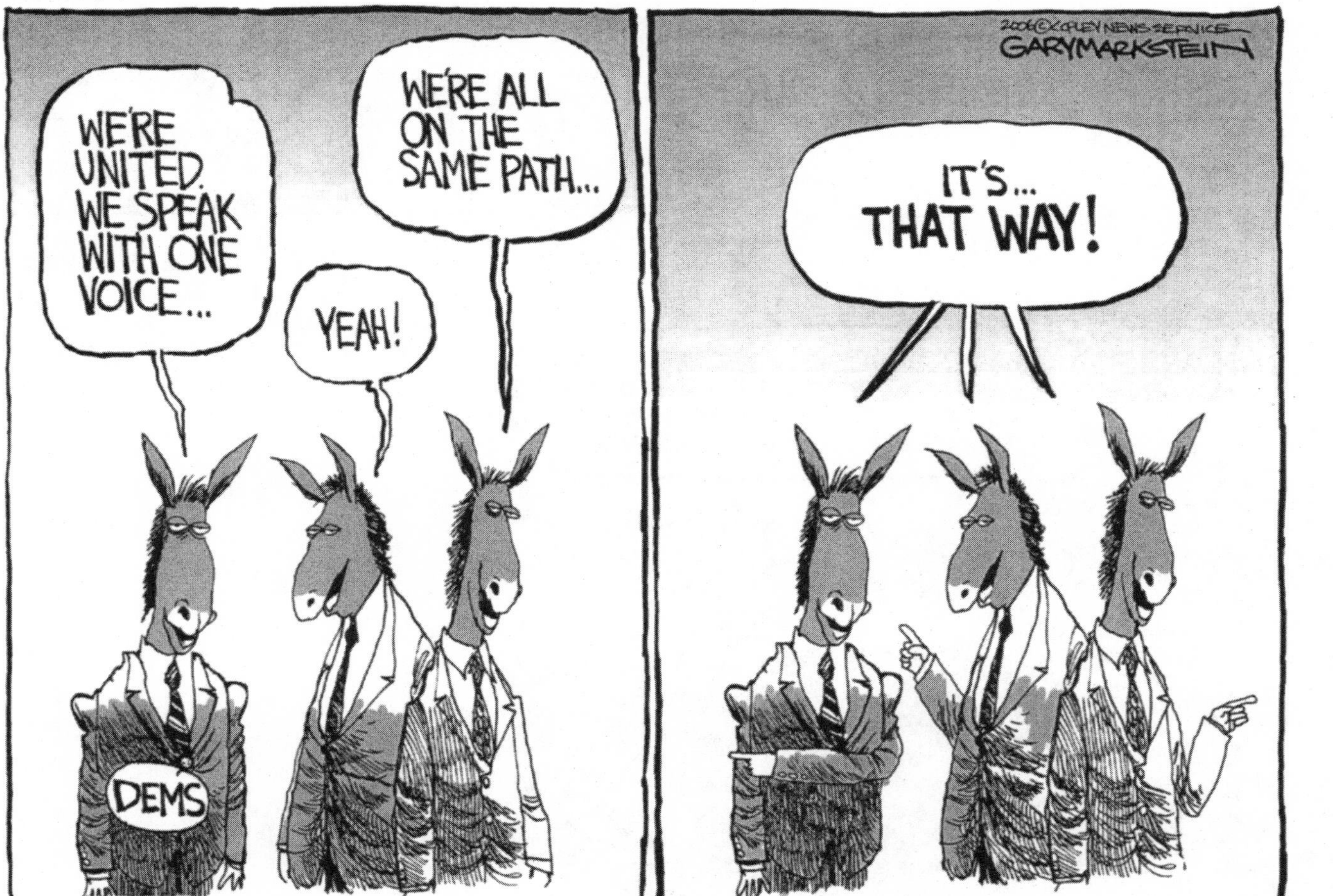
WE'RE UNITED. WE SPEAK WITH ONE VOICE...
YEAH!
WE'RE ALL ON THE SAME PATH...
DEMS
2006©COPLEY NEWS SERVICE
GARYMARKSTEIN
IT'S... THAT WAY!

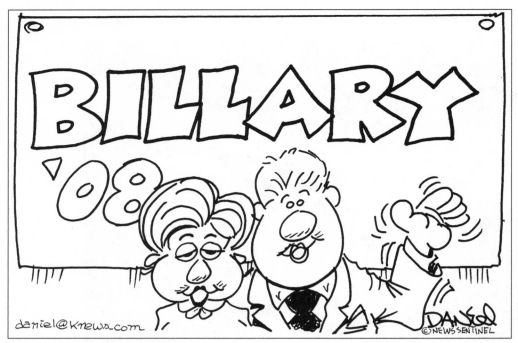

CHARLES DANIEL
Courtesy Knoxville News-Sentinel

CARL MOORE
Courtesy Creators Syndicate

PAUL BERGE
Courtesy Journal Times (Wisc.)

STEVE KELLEY
Courtesy The Times-Picayune (La.)

ALAN VITELLO
Courtesy Greeley Tribune

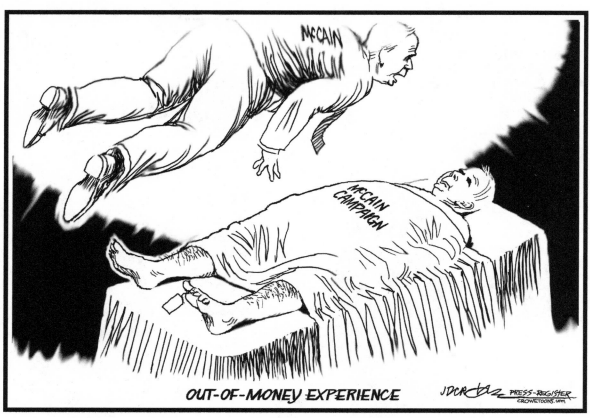

J.D. CROWE
Courtesy Mobile Register

NICK ANDERSON
Courtesy Houston Chronicle

AARON TAYLOR
Courtesy Daily Herald (Utah)

MICHAEL RAMIREZ
Courtesy Investor's Business Daily

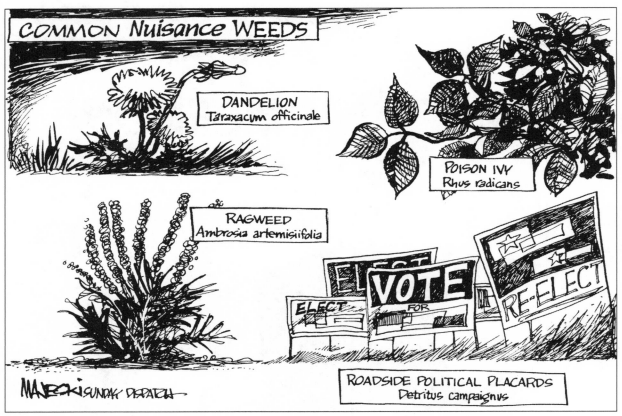

JOE MAJESKI
Courtesy The Sunday Dispatch (Pa.)

## The Clinton Position

JEFF DANZIGER
Courtesy NYTS/CWS

PRESIDENTIAL CANDIDATES' BEST FRIEND

JIM DYKE
Courtesy Jefferson City News-Tribune

JIM HUNT
Courtesy Charlotte Post

PAUL CONRAD
Courtesy Tribune Media Services

# The Bush Administration

Polls showed that 69 percent of the American people disapproved of the way President Bush was handling the Iraq war. Bush staked his legacy on a troop surge, a buildup of some 30,000 troops in the most perilous areas of Iraq, and asked the public to wait until September to make a judgment.

September came, and Gen. David Petraeus delivered his assessment to Congress: the surge was working; given enough time, victory was still possible. Democrats pooh-poohed his report and the far-left called him a liar, but his words seemed to have gained Bush some time.

The sentence of former White House aide Lewis "Scooter" Libby, convicted of obstruction of justice and perjury in the Valerie Plame case, was commuted by President Bush. Atty. Gen. Alberto Gonzales was forced to resign in August. The beginning of the end came when he fired eight U.S. attorneys and then seemed to give evasive answers to a congressional subcommittee investigating the matter. Bush immediately nominated Michael Mukasey, a tough-on-terrorism former federal judge, to replace Gonzales.

Karl Rove, Bush's longtime friend and closest advisor, resigned in August. Vice President Dick Cheney continued to draw fire from critics of the Administration.

BOB ARIAIL
Courtesy The State (S.C.)

JON RICHARDS
Courtesy Albuquerque Journal North

MIKE KEEFE
Courtesy Denver Post

S.C. RAWLS
Courtesy The Citizen

CLAY BENNETT
Courtesy Christian Science Monitor

Those who do not learn from history are doomed to repeat it.

JOHN SHERFFIUS
Courtesy Boulder Camera/
Copley News Service

JIM BORGMAN
Courtesy Cincinnati Enquirer

LINCOLN
AS THE DEATH TOLL CLIMBED

LBJ
AS THE CASUALTIES MOUNTED

DUBYA
AS THE WAR RAGED ON

FRED CURATOLO
Courtesy Edmonton Sun

STEVE BREEN
Courtesy San Diego Union-Tribune

JIM MORIN
Courtesy Miami Herald

CLAY BENNETT
Courtesy Christian Science Monitor

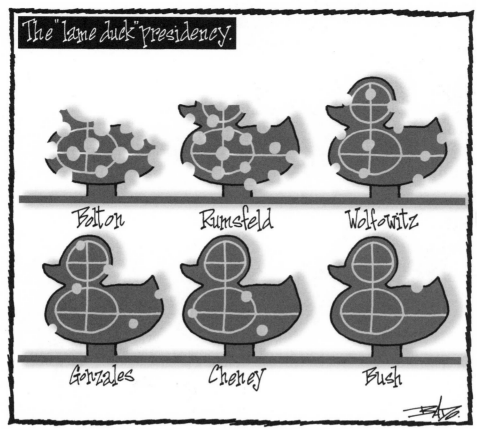

GUY BADEAUX
Courtesy LeDroit (Ottawa)

MIKE PETERS
Courtesy Dayton Daily News

VIC HARVILLE
Courtesy Stephens Media Group

MARK STREETER
Courtesy Savannah Morning News

JIM MORIN
Courtesy Miami Herald

STEPHEN TEMPLETON
Courtesy The Flathead Beacon

JACK HIGGINS
Courtesy Chicago Sun-Times

JUSTIN DeFREITAS
Courtesy Berkeley Daily Planet

JOHN TREVER
Courtesy Albuquerque Journal

DEB MILBRATH
Courtesy CNN AAEC Website

MILT PRIGGEE
Courtesy www.miltpriggee.com

JOSEPH RANK
Courtesy Times-Press Recorder (Calif.)

ALAN J. NASH
Courtesy Gering Courier/
North Platte Bulletin

LINDA BOILEAU
Courtesy State Journal (Ky.)

STEVE EDWARDS
Courtesy St. Louis Journalism Review

NICK ANDERSON
Courtesy Houston Chronicle

JIM LANGE
Courtesy Daily Oklahoman

TOM STIGLICH
Courtesy Northeast Times (Pa.)

ROSS GOSSE
Courtesy Pine Tree Syndicate

MIKE LUCKOVICH
Courtesy Atlanta Constitution

ED STEIN
Courtesy Rocky Mountain News

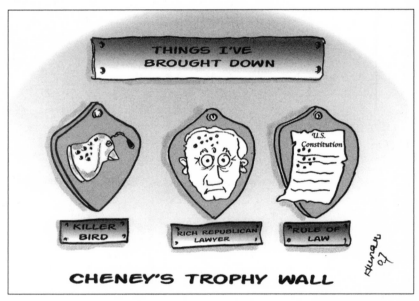

BARRY HUNAU
Courtesy cartoonsbybarry.com

ETTA HULME
Courtesy Fort Worth Star-Telegram

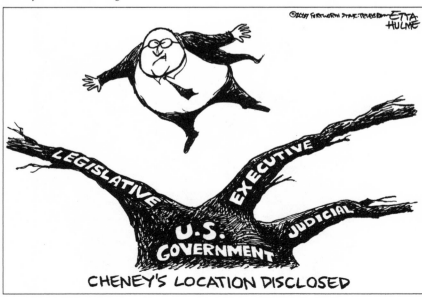

JIM BORGMAN
Courtesy Cincinnati Enquirer

JACK HIGGINS
Courtesy Chicago Sun-Times

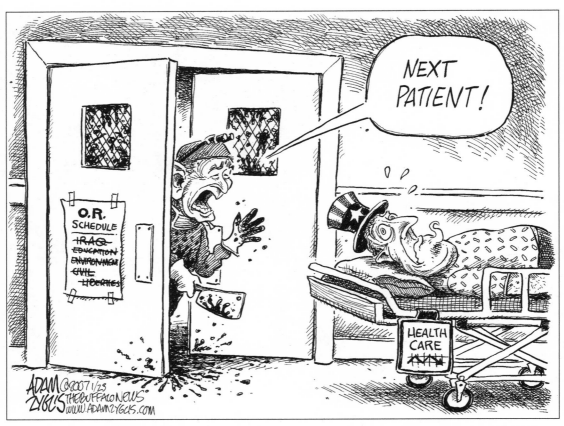

ADAM ZYGLIS
Courtesy Buffalo News

JON RICHARDS
Courtesy Albuquerque Journal North

GEORGE DANBY
Courtesy Bangor Daily News

LARRY KASSELL
Courtesy Silverton Appeal Tribune (Ore.)

JOHN COLE
Courtesy Herald-Sun Newspapers

JIM DYKE
Courtesy Jefferson City News-Tribune

The Budget

JEFF DANZIGER
Courtesy NYTS/CWS

48

JOHN BRANCH
Courtesy San Antonio Express-News

STEVE GREENBERG
Courtesy Ventura County Star

DRAPER HILL
Courtesy Grosse Pointe Pub. Co.

JIM SIERGEY
Courtesy www.jimsiergey.com

RANDY BISH
Courtesy Tribune-Review (Pa.)

# Iraq / Terrorism

Former Iraqi dictator Saddam Hussein was found guilty of a multitude of murders and was hanged just before New Year's Day 2007. Despite objections from lawmakers in both parties and some generals, President Bush sent a surge of additional forces to Iraq. There were some successes, leading to a reduction of violence in Baghdad and in Fallujah, a former hotbed of insurgency. Nevertheless, the Iraqi government's grip on power remained threatened by terrorists and sectarian violence.

Harry Reid, Democratic leader of the Senate, early in 2007 declared the war in Iraq "lost," and sought to find ways to redeploy U.S. troops elsewhere. President Bush continued to urge America to stay the course.

The U.S. ended a 27-year diplomatic freeze during 2007, holding brief talks with Iran. Not much came of the discussions, but the U.S. demanded that Iran stop arming and financing militants who attack U.S. forces, particularly suicide bombers. Fighting continued between Palestinians and Israel, with gunmen attacking border troops and firing rockets into Israeli settlements. Israel returned fire with rockets.

The killing of refugees in Darfur continued as the United Nations continued its inaction.

LUCAS TURNBLOOM
Courtesy Artizans Syndicate

51

NICK ANDERSON
Courtesy Houston Chronicle

JOHN COLE
Courtesy Herald-Sun Newspapers

JOHN LARTER
Courtesy Calgary Sun

S.C. RAWLS
Courtesy The Citizen

53

STEVEN LAIT
Courtesy Oakland Tribune

MIKE PETERS
Courtesy Dayton Daily News

STAN BURDICK
Courtesy Lake Champlain Weekly

DANA SUMMERS
Courtesy Orlando Sentinel

MIKE KEEFE
Courtesy Denver Post

LISA BENSON
Courtesy Washington Post Writers Group

JUSTIN DeFREITAS
Courtesy Berkeley Daily Planet

CHAN LOWE
Courtesy Fort Lauderdale News/
   Sun Sentinel

NATE BEELER
Courtesy Washington Examiner

ED STEIN
Courtesy Rocky Mountain News

DICK LOCHER
Courtesy Chicago Tribune

J.D. CROWE
Courtesy Mobile Register

MIKE LUCKOVICH
Courtesy Atlanta Constitution

JOHN BRANCH
Courtesy San Antonio Express-News

CLAY BENNETT
Courtesy Christian Science Monitor

STEVE LINDSTROM
Courtesy Duluth News-Tribune

MIKE LESTER
Courtesy Rome News Tribune (Ga.)

STEVE LINDSTROM
Courtesy Duluth News-Tribune

DANA SUMMERS
Courtesy Orlando Sentinel

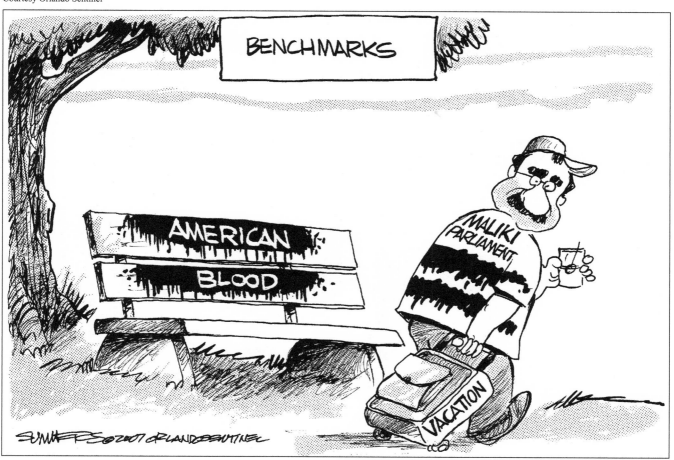

STEVE BREEN
Courtesy San Diego Union-Tribune

WAYNE STROOT
Courtesy Hastings Tribune

ED GAMBLE
Courtesy Florida Times-Union

CHRIS WRIGHT
Courtesy wright-4u@comcast.net

RON ROGERS
Courtesy South Bend Tribune

TIM HARTMAN
Courtesy Beaver County Times (Pa.)

DICK LOCHER
Courtesy Chicago Tribune

64

MILT PRIGGEE
Courtesy www.miltpriggee.com

DICK LOCHER
Courtesy Chicago Tribune

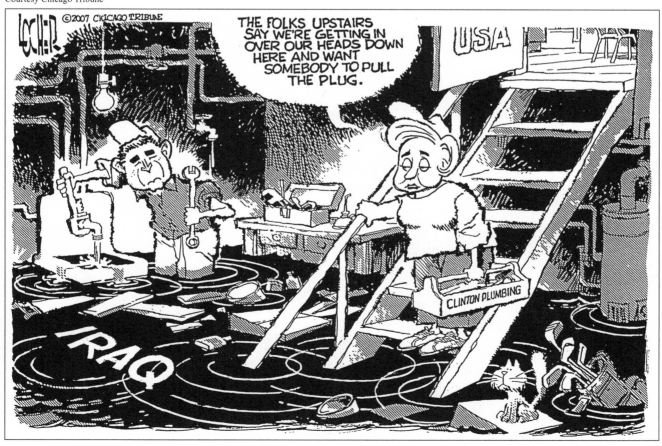

JAKE FULLER
Courtesy Gainesville Sun

BOB ARIAIL
Courtesy The State (S.C.)

JOHN TREVER
Courtesy Albuquerque Journal

MIKE LUCKOVICH
Courtesy Atlanta Constitution

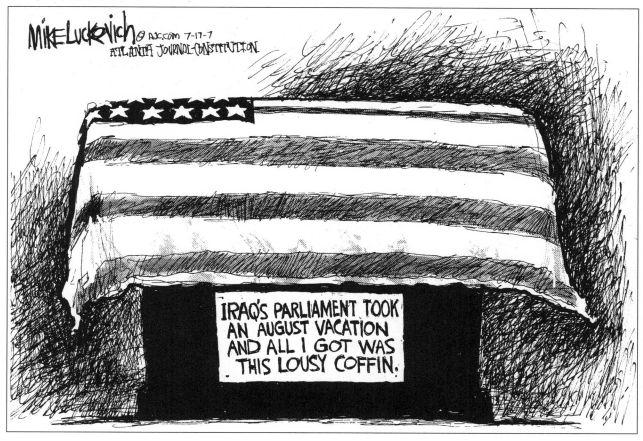

MIKE LESTER
Courtesy Rome News Tribune (Ga.)

MIKE PETERS
Courtesy Dayton Daily News

JOSEPH RANK
Courtesy Times-Press Recorder (Calif.)

BOB GORRELL
Courtesy Creators Syndicate

TERRY C. WISE
Courtesy Ratland Ink Press

GARY VARVEL
Courtesy Indianapolis Star

ANDREW WAHL
Courtesy Wenatchee World (Wash.)

STEPHEN TEMPLETON
Courtesy The Flathead Beacon

JIM LANGE
Courtesy Daily Oklahoman

CHRIS BRITT
Courtesy State Journal-Register (Ill.)

TED RALL
Courtesy Universal Press Syndicate

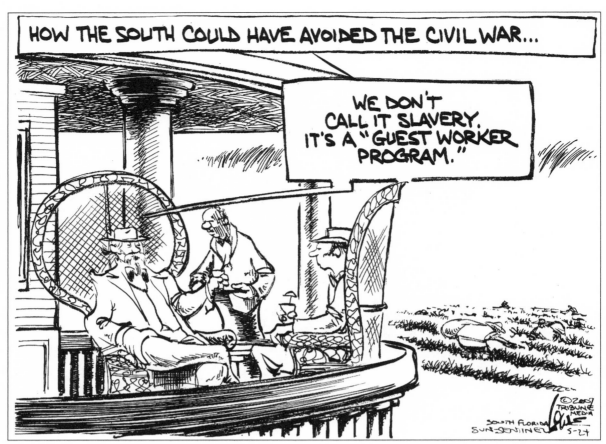

CHAN LOWE
Courtesy Fort Lauderdale News/
Sun Sentinel

LISA BENSON
Courtesy Washington Post Writers Group

# Immigration

A ground swell of public opposition helped kill a Senate immigration reform bill fashioned by an unlikely alliance of liberal Democrats and conservative Republicans.

President Bush strongly endorsed the bill and urged his party to support it, but conservative senators found themselves inundated by telephone calls and emails from constituents calling for its defeat. In the end, the lawmakers voted to continue debate on the bill, effectively killing it. In a remarkable twist, the liberal *New York Times* and conservative radio talk show hosts agreed it was a bad bill.

If it had been enacted, the bill would have allowed the 12 million illegal aliens to remain in the U.S. In addition, it would have left open the doors to many more since there was no real provision to close the borders. Critics insisted the plan amounted to amnesty and would severely burden the country's social services system. Little progress was made during the year in constructing a security fence along the border.

With Congress having failed to make any realistic changes in immigration policy, states began to develop their own laws to deal with the matter.

ED HALL
Courtesy Baker County Press

ED GAMBLE
Courtesy Florida Times-Union

TOM BECK
Courtesy Freeport Journal-Standard (Ill.)

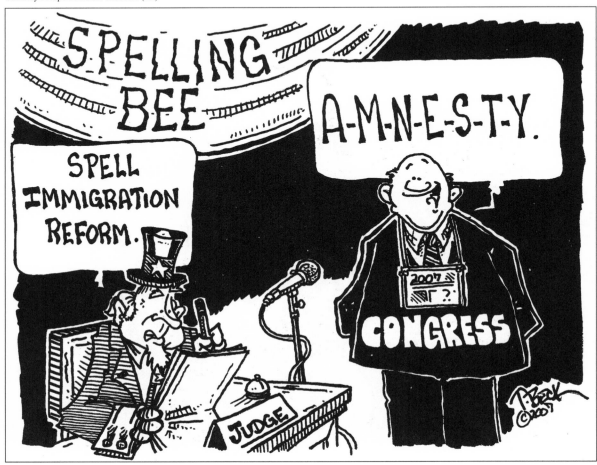

BOB ARIAIL
Courtesy The State (S.C.)

Greetings to Latin America!

JEFF DANZIGER
Courtesy NYTS/CWS

BOB UNELL
Courtesy Kansas City Star

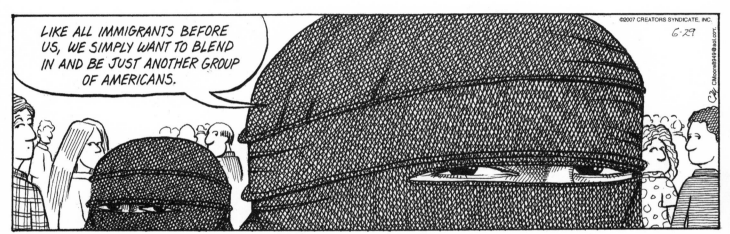

CARL MOORE
Courtesy Creators Syndicate

WALT HANDELSMAN
Courtesy Newsday

JIM DYKE
Courtesy Jefferson City News-Tribune

RICK KOLLINGER
Courtesy Star Democrat (Md.)

THE SPIRIT OF '07

RICHARD WALLMEYER
Courtesy Long Beach Press-Telegram

BILL GARNER
Courtesy Washington Times

© 2007 · THE WASHINGTON TIMES
GARNER 6·20

## WHAT ABOUT AMERICA?

AS YOU READ THIS, ILLEGALS HAVE BEEN
SETTING FIRE TO OUR PRISTINE NATIONAL
FOREST ALONG THE U.S.-MEXICAN BORDER
TO DIVERT THE ATTENTION OF OUR BORDER
AGENTS SO THAT ILLEGALS AND DRUG CARTELS
CAN WALK ACROSS OUR BORDERS.

WHERE ARE OUR U.S. MILITARY? OUR NATIONAL
GUARD? IN IRAQ, SAVING AND PROTECTING THE
PEOPLE OF IRAQ.

WELL, WHAT ABOUT AMERICA?
WHERE IS OUR CONGRESS? OUR HOMELAND SECURITY?
OUR PRESIDENT?...

...SITTING ON THEIR
ASSES!

DANI AGUILA
Courtesy Filipino Reporter

LUCAS TURNBLOOM
Courtesy Artizans Syndicate

ED STEIN
Courtesy Rocky Mountain News

MIKE LESTER
Courtesy Rome News Tribune (Ga.)

MIKE BECKOM
Courtesy Hartsville Messenger

# Congress

In a triumph for the pharmaceutical industry, the U.S. Senate killed legislation that would have allowed consumers to buy prescription drugs from abroad at significant savings over domestic prices. Under the bill, the administration would have been required to certify the safety and effectiveness of imported drugs—a requirement that officials said they could not meet.

Intense public opposition led to the defeat of an immigration bill that would have granted legal status to millions of illegal aliens and set up a guest worker program. Critics called it an amnesty bill and declared that it would overwhelm social services programs across the U.S.

Both the House and the Senate passed bills calling for beginning withdrawal of U.S. troops from Iraq by October 1, 2007, with a stated goal of having all troops out six months later. Bush vetoed the legislation, and proponents could not muster the votes to override the President.

Former Ohio Rep. Bob Ney was sentenced to thirty months in prison for conspiracy, Rep. William Jefferson, a Louisiana Democrat, was indicted on federal charges of racketeering, and Republican Sen. Larry Craig pleaded guilty to a charge of disorderly conduct after an incident in an airport men's room.

DICK LOCHER
Courtesy Chicago Tribune

SANDY HUFFAKER
Courtesy caglecartoons.com

CHARLIE HALL
Courtesy Rhode Island News Group

ROGER SCHILLERSTROM
Courtesy Crain Communications

JEFF PARKER
Courtesy Florida Today

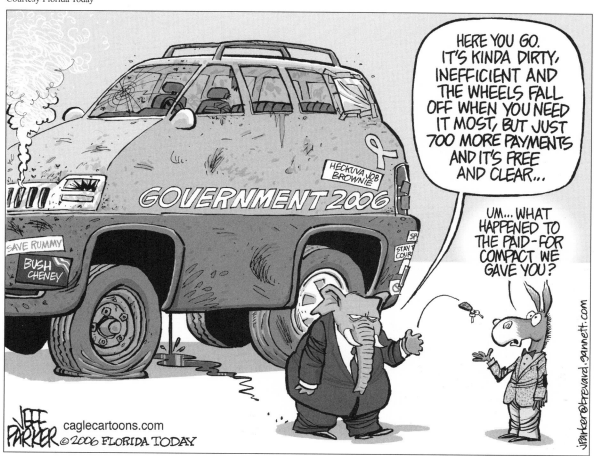

JOHN AUCHTER
Courtesy Grand Rapids Business Journal

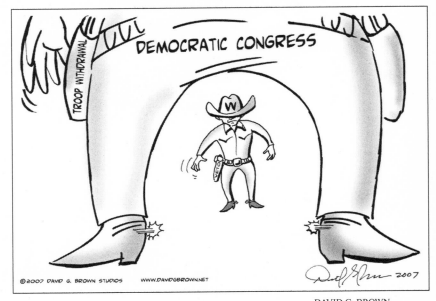

DAVID G. BROWN
Courtesy Los Angeles Sentinel

SCOTT-ALLEN PIERSON
Courtesy Viking News (N.J.)

WAYNE STROOT
Courtesy Hastings Tribune

STEVE McBRIDE
Courtesy Independence Daily Reporter

ED GAMBLE
Courtesy Florida Times-Union

BOB GORRELL
Courtesy Creators Syndicate

DAVID HITCH
Courtesy Worcester Telegram & Gazette

RICHARD CROWSON
Courtesy Wichita Eagle

ETTA HULME
Courtesy Fort Worth Star-Telegram

PAUL COMBS
Courtesy Tribune Media Services

STEVE McBRIDE
Courtesy Independence Daily Reporter

VAUGHN LARSON
Courtesy Wisconsin News Press

STEVEN LAIT
Courtesy Oakland Tribune

JIM LANGE
Courtesy Daily Oklahoman

STEPHEN TEMPLETON
Courtesy The Flathead Beacon

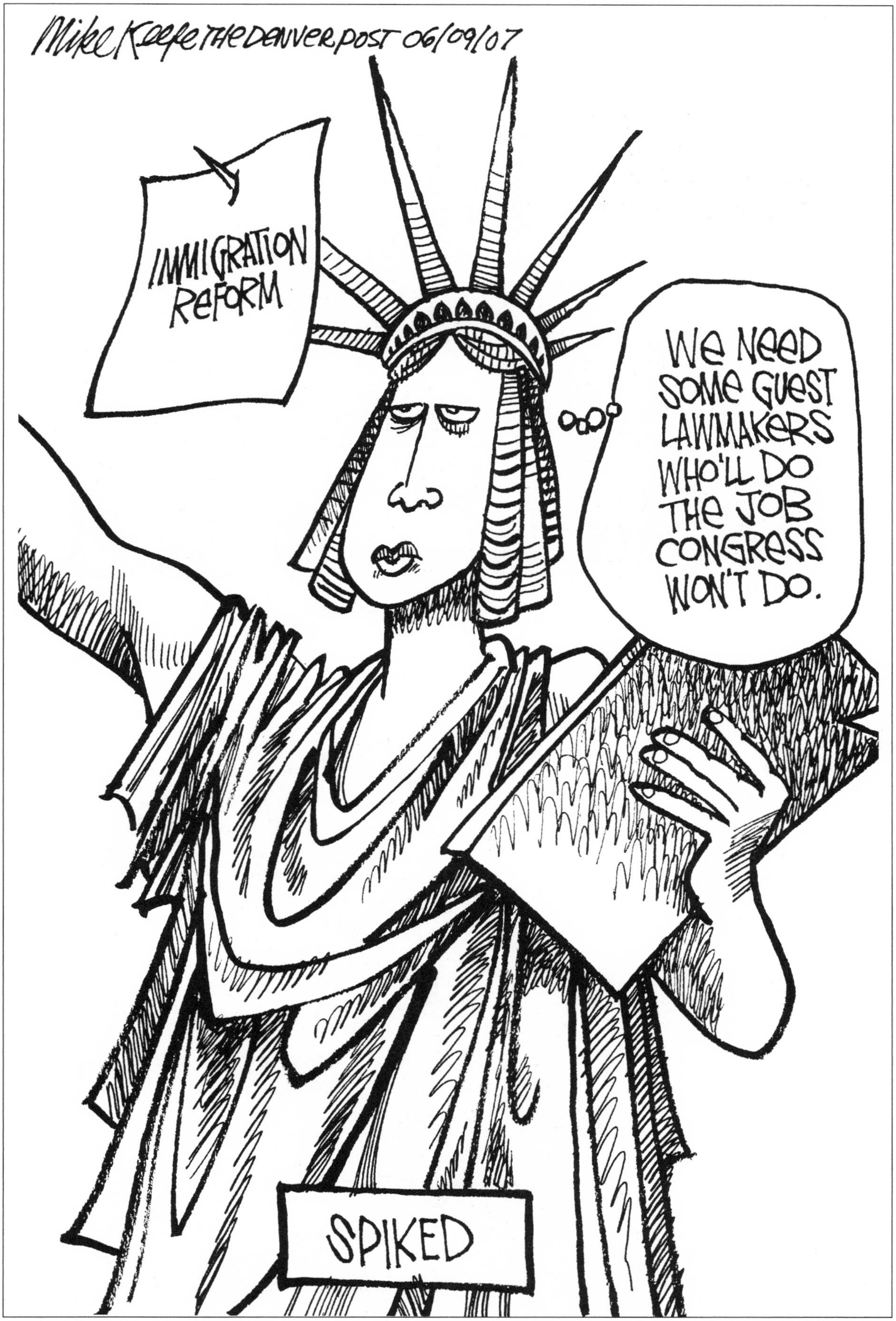
Mike Keefe The Denver Post 06/09/07
IMMIGRATION REFORM
We need some guest lawmakers who'll do the job Congress won't do.
SPIKED

MIKE KEEFE
Courtesy Denver Post

JAKE FULLER
Courtesy Gainesville Sun

MICHAEL RAMIREZ
Courtesy Investor's Business Daily

CASH COW

PAUL CONRAD
Courtesy Tribune Media Services

JERRY BARNETT
Courtesy Boonville Standard (Ind.)

TOM STIGLICH
Courtesy Northeast Times (Pa.)

MICHAEL RAMIREZ
Courtesy Investor's Business Daily

# Crime

Prosecutors dropped all charges against three Duke University lacrosse players accused of sexually assaulting a stripper at a team party, declaring the players were innocent victims of a "tragic rush to accuse" by an overreaching District Attorney Mike Nifong.

A 23-year-old resident alien from South Korea shot and killed 33 people on the campus of Virginia Tech University in a massacre that shocked the nation. After opening fire in a dormitory and a classroom building, the gunman committed suicide. Professional wrestling star Chris Benoit killed his wife and young son and then himself in a bizarre murder-suicide. It was suspected that anabolic steroids could have been involved.

Atlanta Falcons quarterback Michael Vick pleaded guilty to charges of being implicated in organized gambling on dogfights, and O.J. Simpson was charged with armed robbery in a Las Vegas hotel incident. Simpson claimed he was trying to recover property stolen from him. Simpson's notorious book *If I Did It* went on sale.

Protestors flocked to the small town of Jena, Louisiana, after six black youths, dubbed the Jena 6, were charged with beating a white student unconscious.

KEVIN SIERS
Courtesy Charlotte Observer

MIKE LUCKOVICH
Courtesy Atlanta Constitution

NATE BEELER
Courtesy Washington Examiner

PAUL FELL
Courtesy Lincoln Journal Star

ROB ROGERS
Courtesy Pittsburgh Post-Gazette

JIM HOPE
Courtesy Culpepper News (Va.)

CHUCK ASAY
Courtesy Creators Syndicate

DOUG MacGREGOR
Courtesy Fort Myers News-Press

WALT HANDELSMAN
Courtesy Newsday

ROB ROGERS
Courtesy Pittsburgh Post-Gazette

BUSTED
IN
VEGAS...

STEVE BREEN
Courtesy San Diego Union-Tribune

DAVID DONAR
Courtesy Macomb Daily (Miss.)

TIM JACKSON
Courtesy Chicago Defender

RICHARD BARTHOLOMEW
Courtesy Seattle Times

MISFIRE

DAVID HITCH
Courtesy Worcester Telegram & Gazette

DENNIS DRAUGHON
Courtesy Fayetteville Observer/
Durham News

JOHN COLE
Courtesy Herald-Sun Newspapers

RICHARD WALLMEYER
Courtesy Long Beach Press-Telegram

CHRIS BRITT
Courtesy State Journal-Register (Ill.)

GARY VARVEL
Courtesy Indianapolis Star

BOB ARIAIL
Courtesy The State (S.C.)

LINDA BOILEAU
Courtesy State Journal (Ky.)

RICHARD WALLMEYER
Courtesy Long Beach Press-Telegram

CHRIS BRITT
Courtesy State Journal-Register (Ill.)

KARL WIMER
Courtesy Denver Business Journal

MILT PRIGGEE
Courtesy www.miltpriggee.com

# The Economy

2007 was a roller coaster year for the American economy. In February, the stock market experienced its worst one-day decline since the 2001 attacks. The market rebounded, however, and by summer the Dow Jones Industrial Average hit a record 14,000. But by August the Dow had plunged again to 13,000. Markets around the world were also affected, but economists generally agreed that the global economy remained fairly healthy—for the moment.

The stock market received a shot in the arm on September 18 when the Federal Reserve trimmed 50 basis points off the cost of borrowing. The Dow immediately soared, ending the day up 335 points. Strong economic growth elsewhere helped many U.S. companies reap big profits from sales abroad. Furthermore, a generally weak American dollar made U.S. goods cheaper in overseas market.

Many experts, however, saw the possibility of a recession sometime in 2008. With rising gasoline prices fueled by $80-a-barrel oil and mortgage foreclosures soaring because of shaky sub-prime loans, economic prospects looked tenuous at best.

The federal deficit trended sharply lower as the year wore on. During the first nine months growth in revenues continued to outpace growth in spending.

SCOTT STANTIS
Courtesy Birmingham News

CHAN LOWE
Courtesy Fort Lauderdale News/
Sun Sentinel

JOHN RILEY
Courtesy rileycartoons.com

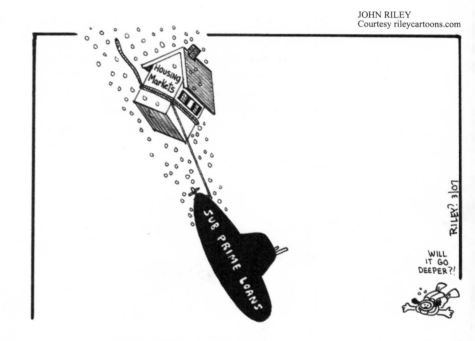

DANIEL FENECH
Courtesy Saline Reporter

JAMES CASCIARI
Courtesy Vero Beach Press Journal

RON ROGERS
Courtesy South Bend Tribune

JIM MORIN
Courtesy Miami Herald

PEDRO MOLINA
Courtesy CWS

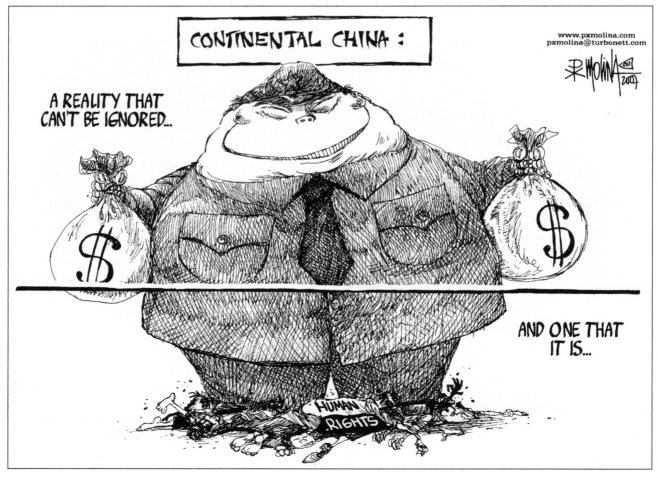

ALAN VITELLO
Courtesy Greeley Tribune

BOB LANG
Courtesy Editorial Services

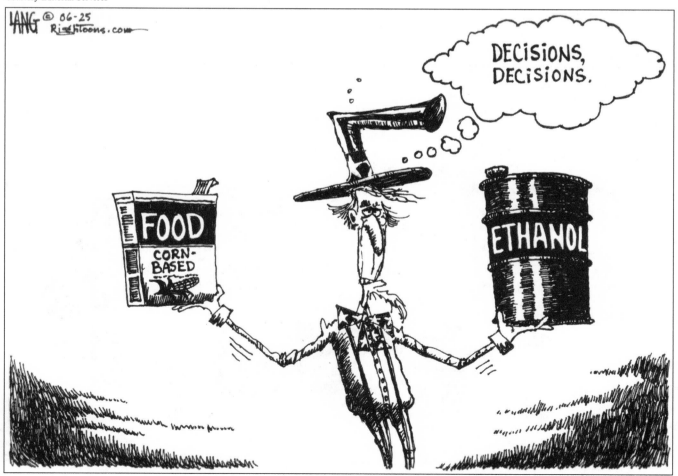

ERIC SMITH
Courtesy Annapolis Capital-Gazette

LARRY WRIGHT
Courtesy Detroit News

S.W. PARRA
Courtesy Fresno Bee

ROSS GOSSE
Courtesy Pine Tree Syndicate

WILLIAM L. FLINT
Courtesy Dallas Morning News

JAMES CASCIARI
Courtesy Vero Beach Press Journal

SANDY HUFFAKER
Courtesy caglecartoons.com

RICKY NOBILE
Courtesy Hattiesburg American

BOB UNELL
Courtesy Kansas City Star

ETTA HULME
Courtesy Fort Worth Star-Telegram

DENNIS DRAUGHON
Courtesy Fayetteville Observer/
Durham News

TIM HARTMAN
Courtesy Beaver County Times (Pa.)

NEIL GRAHAME
Courtesy Spencer Newspapers

PAUL CONRAD
Courtesy Tribune Media Services

JOE HOFFECKER
Courtesy Cincinnati Business Courier

LUCAS TURNBLOOM
Courtesy Artizans Syndicate

118

WILLIAM L. FLINT
Courtesy Dallas Morning News

JESSE SPRINGER
Courtesy Eugene Register-Guard

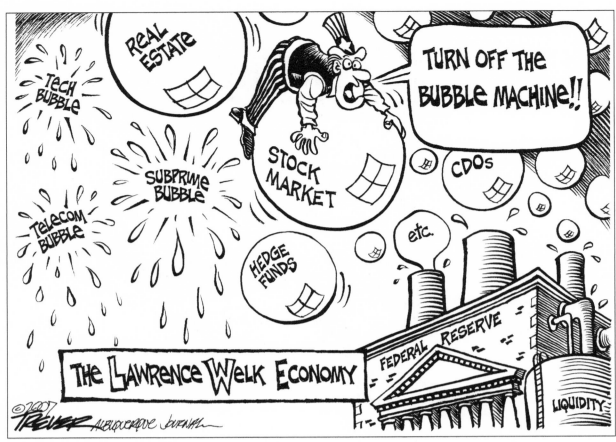

JOHN TREVER
Courtesy Albuquerque Journal

JOE HELLER
Courtesy Green Bay Press-Gazette

# Foreign Affairs

Russian leader Vladimir Putin appeared to be moving toward a revival of the Cold War, announcing new missile tests and harshly condemning the United States on a variety of fronts.

President Hugo Chavez of Venezuela was granted free rein by voters to make changes by presidential decree, moving that country toward a full-fledged dictatorship. One of Chavez's first moves under the new authority was to nationalize foreign oil companies, telecommunications, and electric utilities. He also instituted tighter controls on the press.

North Korea and the U.S. reached an agreement to shut down, seal, and ultimately disable the rogue nation's nuclear facilities. North Korea did not indicate when it might be willing to give up its nuclear arsenal. Iran, on the other hand, has not conceded one inch amid international pressure to give up its nuclear enrichment program.

Nicolas Sarkozy, a pro-American conservative, was elected president of France with a mandate to chart a new course for the economically sluggish nation. Meanwhile, Mexico, a harsh critic of U.S. immigration policies, continued to deport thousands of immigrants to their countries of origin.

Rumors continued to surface that Cuban dictator Fidel Castro was dying, but no one seemed able to confirm that as fact.

POL GALVEZ
Courtesy Philippine News

* MT. 'MAKILING' IS A NOTABLE MOUNTAIN IN THE PHILIPPINES

STEVE McBRIDE
Courtesy Independence Daily Reporter

TIM JACKSON
Courtesy Chicago Defender

122

BILL GARNER
Courtesy Washington Times

CHARLES DANIEL
Courtesy Knoxville News-Sentinel

FRED CURATOLO
Courtesy Edmonton Sun

GARY MARKSTEIN
Courtesy Copley News Service

JUSTIN DeFREITAS
Courtesy Berkeley Daily Planet

POL GALVEZ
Courtesy Philippine News

CARL MOORE
Courtesy Creators Syndicate

125

PEDRO MOLINA
Courtesy CWS

JOHN TREVER
Courtesy Albuquerque Journal

# Health / Environment

A panel of some of the world's leading climate scientists concluded that global warming has begun, is "very likely" being caused by man, and will be unstoppable for centuries. Using the strongest language yet on the issue, the group said temperatures and sea level will continue to rise, no matter how well humans control pollution.

The U.S. Supreme Court rebuked the Bush Administration for inaction on the global warming front, declaring that greenhouse gasses are pollutants under the Clear Air Act.

An earthquake spawned a tsunami that hit the Solomon Islands, killing thirteen, and Japan was hit by a 6.8 earthquake that left tens of thousands without power or water. A nuclear power plant in Japan suffered damage and was shut down. A 7.9 temblor shook the coast of Peru, killing hundreds and injuring hundreds more. At least 200 were buried in the rubble of a church where they were attending a special service.

It was another record year for wildfires in the United States, with Georgia suffering its worst conflagrations in fifty years. Oklahoma, Kansas, and Texas were hit by weeks of flooding while much of the West endured record-setting heat and the Southeast experienced drought. It was almost as if Mother Nature had run amok.

ROGER SCHILLERSTROM
Courtesy Crain Communications

MIKE KEEFE
Courtesy Denver Post

JEFF DANZIGER
Courtesy NYTS/CWS

PAUL COMBS
Courtesy Tribune Media Services

LARRY WRIGHT
Courtesy Detroit News

129

RICHARD WALLMEYER
Courtesy Long Beach Press-Telegram

CLAY BENNETT
Courtesy Christian Science Monitor

GARY MARKSTEIN
Courtesy Copley News Service

JEFF DANZIGER
Courtesy NYTS/CWS

TOM STIGLICH
Courtesy Northeast Times (Pa.)

CHUCK ASAY
Courtesy Creators Syndicate

DON LANDGREN, JR.
Courtesy The Landmark (Mass.)

DAVE SATTLER
Courtesy Lafayette Journal Courier (Ind.)

JIM BORGMAN
Courtesy Cincinnati Enquirer

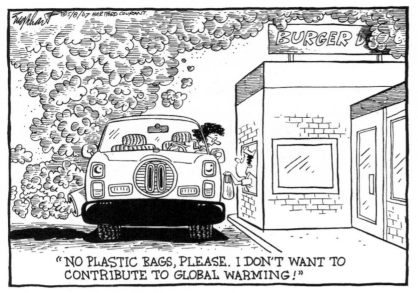

"NO PLASTIC BAGS, PLEASE. I DON'T WANT TO CONTRIBUTE TO GLOBAL WARMING!"

BOB ENGLEHART
Courtesy Hartford Courant

WATCH LESS TELEVISION... EXERCISE MORE... EAT HEALTHIER...

I LIKED IT BETTER BEFORE PARENTAL CONTROL CHIPS...

DANIEL FENECH
Courtesy Saline Reporter

ANN CLEAVES
Courtesy Ann Cleaves

HOW MUCH HEALTH CAN YOU AFFORD?

UNINSURED
WATER  ASPIRIN

HMO APPROVAL REQUIRED FIRST

DELUXE CARE

JAMES CASCIARI
Courtesy Vero Beach Press Journal

WALT HANDELSMAN
Courtesy Newsday

BOB LANG
Courtesy Editorial Services

RICK McKEE
Courtesy Augusta Chronicle

ED STEIN
Courtesy Rocky Mountain News

STEVE GREENBERG
Courtesy Ventura County Star

FRED CURATOLO
Courtesy Edmonton Sun

JOE HOFFECKER
Courtesy Cincinnati Business Courier

ROGER SCHILLERSTROM
Courtesy Crain Communications

MIKE GRASTON
Courtesy Windsor Star (Can.)

SCOTT STANTIS
Courtesy Birmingham News

JAMES CASCIARI
Courtesy Vero Beach Press Journal

LARRY WRIGHT
Courtesy Detroit News

# Media / Entertainment

Troubled pop singer Britney Spears checked in and out of rehabilitation centers several times during year while at the same time battling an ex-spouse for custody of their children. Following a series of run-ins with paparazzi, the one-time teen idol raised eyebrows by shaving her head.

Entertainer Rosie O'Donnell frequently made headlines as well. For several weeks she found herself in a feud with tycoon Donald Trump over . . . well, it was difficult to say exactly why. Rosie went too far when she made inflammatory remarks about the 9/11 attacks and the war in Iraq. As a result, she lost her seat on Barbara Walters' television talk show "The View."

Another talk show icon, Don Imus, was sacked by CBS Radio for making racial comments about the championship Rutgers University girls basketball team. He made numerous apologies for his remarks, but advertisers bolted and he was gone. He later sued CBS over his departure and announced plans for another show. Katie Couric was named anchor for "The CBS Evening News," but was plagued by low ratings.

Paris Hilton, heir to the Hilton Hotels fortune, made scandal sheet news with a variety of questionable actions and spent several days in jail.

CHARLIE HALL
Courtesy Rhode Island News Group

The Britney Effect.

TERRY C. WISE
Courtesy Ratland Ink Press

PETER K. EVANS
Courtesy Islander News (Fla.)

TONY BAYER
Courtesy The News-Dispatch (Ind.)

RICK McKEE
Courtesy Augusta Chronicle

JOE HELLER
Courtesy Green Bay Press-Gazette

MIKE LESTER
Courtesy Rome News Tribune (Ga.)

VIC HARVILLE
Courtesy Stephens Media Group

JIMMY MARGULIES
Courtesy The Record (N.J.)

ELIZABETH BRICQUET
Courtesy Kingsport Times-News (Tenn.)

AARON TAYLOR
Courtesy Daily Herald (Utah)

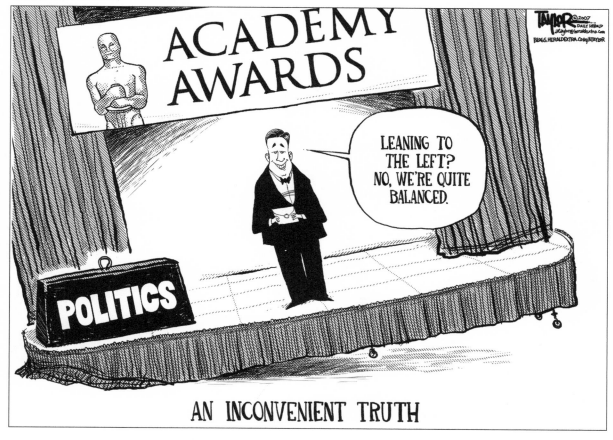

# VIDEO CLIP OF JOHN EDWARDS ARRANGING HIS HAIR

# VIDEO CLIP OF ANN COULTER ARRANGING HERS

KEVIN SIERS
Courtesy Charlotte Observer

MICHAEL RAMIREZ
Courtesy Investor's Business Daily

THE ANCHOR

DANA SUMMERS
Courtesy Orlando Sentinel

MIKE THOMPSON
Courtesy Detroit Free Press

CHARLES DANIEL
Courtesy Knoxville News-Sentinel

SANDY HUFFAKER
Courtesy caglecartoons.com

JIM DYKE
Courtesy Jefferson City News-Tribune

THE TRIFLE TOWER

ROB SMITH, JR.
Courtesy DBR Media

DICK LOCHER
Courtesy Chicago Tribune

149

HAP PITKIN
Courtesy Boulder Camera

GENE HERNDON
Courtesy Noblesville Daily Times (Ind.)

# Society

In downtown Minneapolis on August 1, an interstate highway bridge loaded with rush-hour traffic collapsed and fell more than 60 feet into the Mississippi River. The bridge carried an average of more than 140,000 vehicles a day, which made it Minnesota's busiest bridge. Divers searched for days for bodies buried under the massive debris, but the death toll appeared remarkably low: less than 20.

The world's largest toy company, Mattel Inc., recalled almost a million Chinese-made toys because they may have contained lead, then acknowledged they had acted too hastily. Nevertheless, the recall added to heightening concerns about the safety of other Chinese imports.

Six coal miners were trapped underground near Huntington, Utah, after a massive cave-in. After ten days of efforts to reach the men, another tunnel collapsed, killing three rescue workers and effectively ending the rescue operation.

The last book in the celebrated Harry Potter series hit the bookstores in July. Author J.K. Rowling's first six books in the series have sold more than 325 million copies.

MILT PRIGGEE
Courtesy www.miltpriggee.com

GEORGE DANBY
Courtesy Bangor Daily News

IRENE JOSLIN
Courtesy The Republic (Ind.)

JOHN AUCHTER
Courtesy Grand Rapids Business Journal

STEVE KELLEY
Courtesy The Times-Picayune (La.)

GERALD L. GARDEN
Courtesy UTP Voice (Calif.)

TOM BECK
Courtesy Freeport Journal-Standard (Ill.)

CHRIS WRIGHT
Courtesy wright-4u@comcast.net

MARK STREETER
Courtesy Savannah Morning News

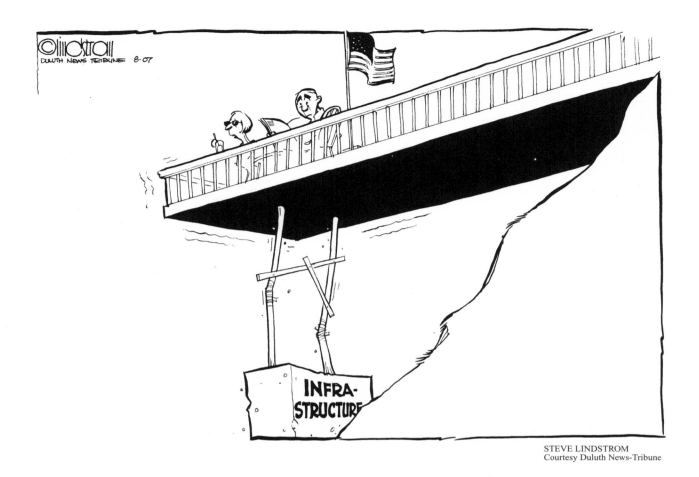

STEVE LINDSTROM
Courtesy Duluth News-Tribune

JOE MAJESKI
Courtesy The Times-Leader (Pa.)

S.W. PARRA
Courtesy Fresno Bee

JIM BUSH
Courtesy Providence Journal (R.I.)

MIKE PETERS
Courtesy Dayton Daily News

JOSEPH O'MAHONEY
Courtesy Patriot Ledger (Mass.)

MIKE THOMPSON
Courtesy Detroit Free Press

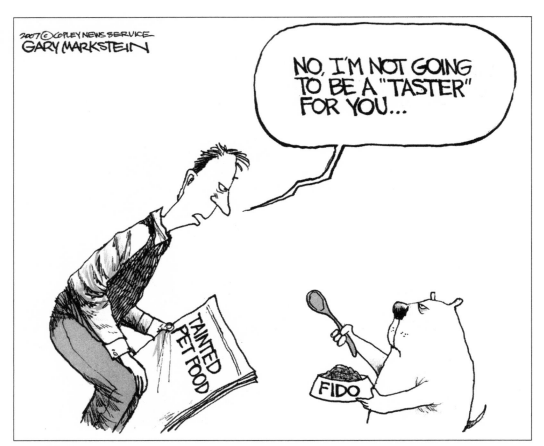

GARY MARKSTEIN
Courtesy Copley News Service

NICK ANDERSON
Courtesy Houston Chronicle

SCOTT STANTIS
Courtesy Birmingham News

CHARLIE HALL
Courtesy Rhode Island News Group

DEB MILBRATH
Courtesy CNN AAEC Website

DON LANDGREN, JR.
Courtesy The Landmark (Mass.)

AARON TAYLOR
Courtesy Daily Herald (Utah)

JOHN SHERFFIUS
Courtesy Boulder Camera/
Copley News Service

MALCOLM MAYES
Courtesy Edmonton Journal

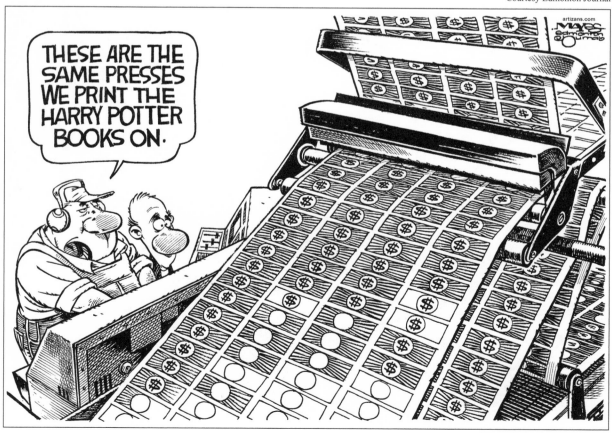

ROY PETERSON
Courtesy Vancouver Sun

MIKE GRASTON
Courtesy Windsor Star (Can.)

WILLIAM L. FLINT
Courtesy Dallas Morning News

SHANE JOHNSON
Courtesy Artizans Media Syndicate

ANNETTE BALESTERI
Courtesy Antioch News

TIM HARTMAN
Courtesy Beaver County Times (Pa.)

NICK ANDERSON
Courtesy Houston Chronicle

CHUCK ASAY
Courtesy Creators Syndicate

DAVID HITCH
Courtesy Worcester Telegram & Gazette

DOUGLAS REGALIA
Courtesy Contra Costa Newspaper Group

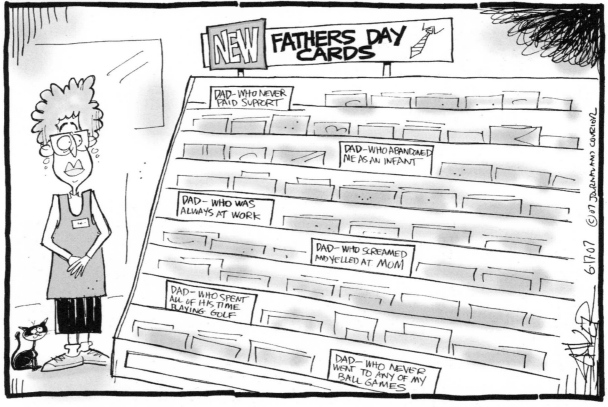

DAVE SATTLER
Courtesy Lafayette Journal Courier (Ind.)

# Sports

On August 4, 2007, Barry Bonds slammed his 755th home run to tie Hank Aaron's major league baseball record. The crowd stood and cheered the feat, but there were boos mixed in as well. Bonds has long been accused of using illegal steroids as his home runs piled up. But he has steadfastly denied using any performance-enhancing drugs.

Several other potential record-breakers find themselves under a similar cloud, and major league baseball is pondering how record books should handle the issue. Bonds hit number 756 on August 7 to become the new home run king.

The almost unstoppable Tiger Woods won his third straight Bridgestone International golf tournament. A week later he captured the Professional Golfers Association title to run his career total of major championships to thirteen.

Kentucky Derby winner Barbaro was put down after complications developed following his gruesome breakdown at the 2006 Preakness. It was the end of an eight-month ordeal that elicited an outpouring of support from across the country. A series of setbacks proved too much for the gallant colt.

J.D. CROWE
Courtesy Mobile Register

ED GAMBLE
Courtesy Florida Times-Union

WILL O'TOOLE
Courtesy Home News & Tribune (N.J.)

BOB GORRELL
Courtesy Creators Syndicate

ED HALL
Courtesy Baker County Press

NEIL GRAHAME
Courtesy Spencer Newspapers

RICHARD CROWSON
Courtesy Wichita Eagle

DOUG MacGREGOR
Courtesy Fort Myers News-Press

AARON TAYLOR
Courtesy Daily Herald (Utah)

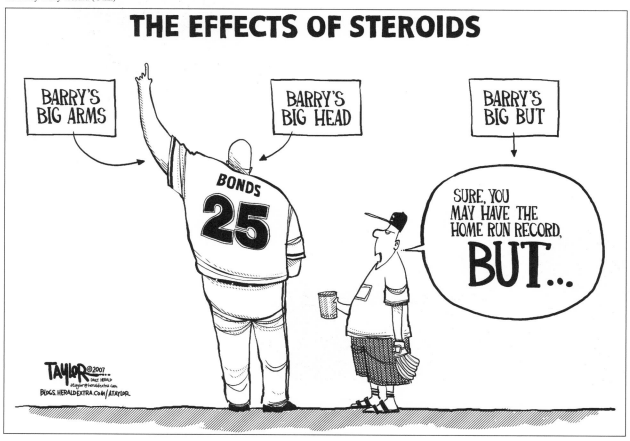

PAUL FELL
Courtesy Lincoln Journal Star

JOHN R. ROSE
Courtesy Byrd Newspapers/
Daily News Record (Va.)

RANAN LURIE
Courtesy Cartoonews, Inc.

MICHAEL RAMIREZ
Courtesy Investor's Business Daily

JOHN COLE
Courtesy Herald-Sun Newspapers

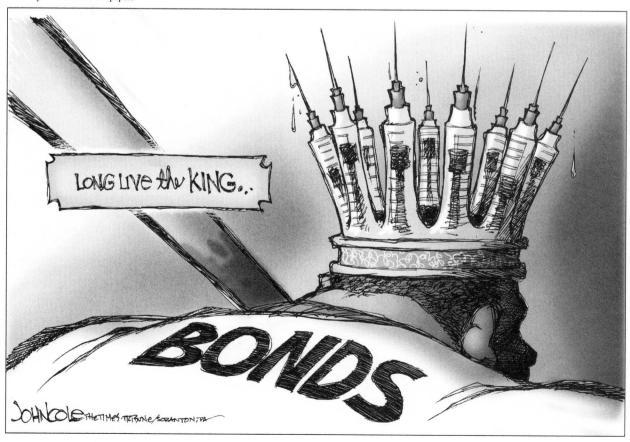

PEDRO MOLINA
Courtesy CWS

JIM BORGMAN
Courtesy Cincinnati Enquirer

# Space / Air Travel

Seven astronauts climbed aboard a patched up *Atlantis* in the spring for the first space shuttle flight of the year. The mission was to continue building the international space station. The flight was held up, however, by a damaging hailstorm and a lurid love triangle. NASA astronaut Lisa Nowak was arrested for an alleged plot to kidnap a rival for a shuttle pilot's affections.

The space shuttle *Endeavor,* carrying teacher/astronaut Barbara Morgan, was damaged during liftoff on a later mission to rendezvous with the international space station. The damage was not life-threatening, and the spaceship returned to earth safely.

Astronauts discovered a planet, known as 581 c, outside the solar system that is potentially inhabitable, with Earth-like temperatures. The discovery was seen as a major step in the search for other life in the universe.

After five major bankruptcies and billions of dollars in losses over the past six years, the airlines finally experienced an upturn and expect to earn big profits in 2007 and 2008. But passengers may not be a lot better off. Flights completed on time in 2007 dropped to 71 percent, the lowest in twenty years.

All in all, air travel remained an unpleasant, stressful experience for millions of Americans.

S.W. PARRA
Courtesy Fresno Bee

STEVE KELLEY
Courtesy The Times-Picayune (La.)

BOB ARIAIL
Courtesy The State (S.C.)

PAUL FELL
Courtesy Lincoln Journal Star

JEFF PARKER
Courtesy Florida Today

ROY PETERSON
Courtesy Vancouver Sun

STEVE NEASE
Courtesy Toronto Sun

MALCOLM MAYES
Courtesy Edmonton Journal

# Canada

Canada unveiled a major border security initiative and said it will spend more than $368 million over the next five years to protect it from terrorist, economic, and environmental threats. Prime Minister Stephen Harper, amid criticism of not paying enough attention to needs at home, announced a $172 million reconstruction aid package for Afghanistan.

Parliament refused to extend anti-terrorism laws that had the strong support of Harper. Following 9/11, Canada had enacted laws to help identify and detain suspected terrorists, but opposition leader Stephane Dion insisted they were an unnecessary infringement on civil liberties.

Canada announced plans for an Arctic army training center and a deepwater port during a trip intended to assert sovereignty over the region. Denmark, however, staked its own claim to the area by sending a scientific expedition. The U.S. launched an exploratory mission toward the Arctic to map the sea floor off Alaska, but denied it was actively joining the Arctic competition.

Russia joined in by sending submarines to plant flags under the North Pole. The U.S. and Norway also have competing claims in the vast region, where a study suggests as much as 25 percent of the world's undiscovered oil and gas could be hidden.

JOHN LARTER
Courtesy Calgary Sun

HARPER'S NEW 'SUMMER TIME' ARCTIC PATROL BOATS SEND A CLEAR MESSAGE TO THE U.S. AND RUSSIA...

TAKE OFF EH!

ARCTIC PATROL

...artizans.com

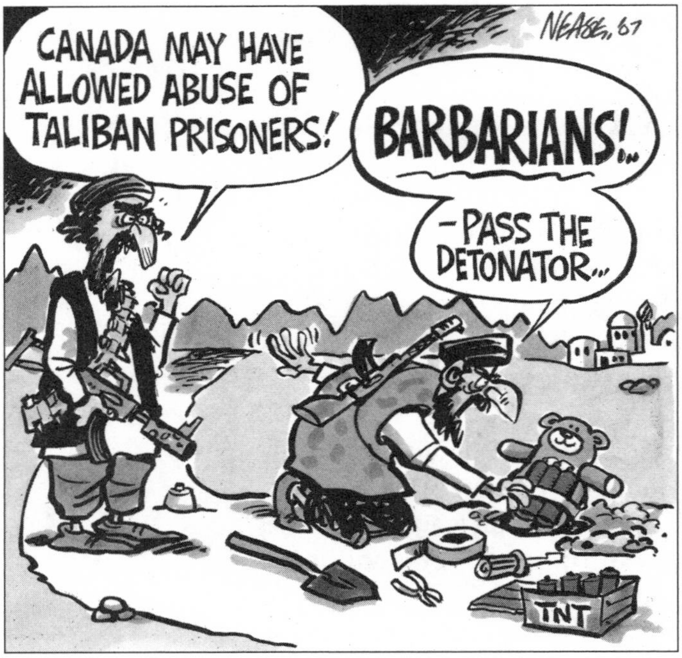
NEASE, '07
CANADA MAY HAVE ALLOWED ABUSE OF TALIBAN PRISONERS!
BARBARIANS!..
-PASS THE DETONATOR...
TNT

STEVE NEASE
Courtesy Toronto Sun

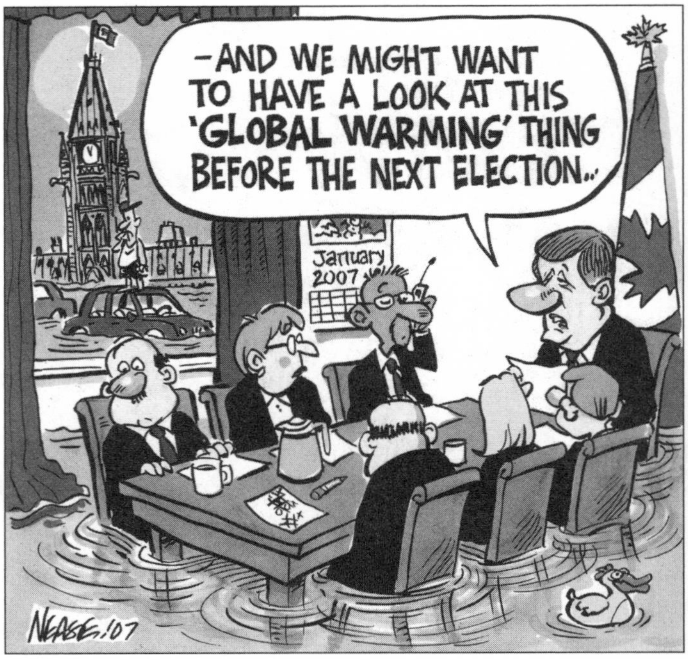
-AND WE MIGHT WANT TO HAVE A LOOK AT THIS 'GLOBAL WARMING' THING BEFORE THE NEXT ELECTION..
January 2007
NEASE, '07

STEVE NEASE
Courtesy Toronto Sun

JOHN LARTER
Courtesy Calgary Sun

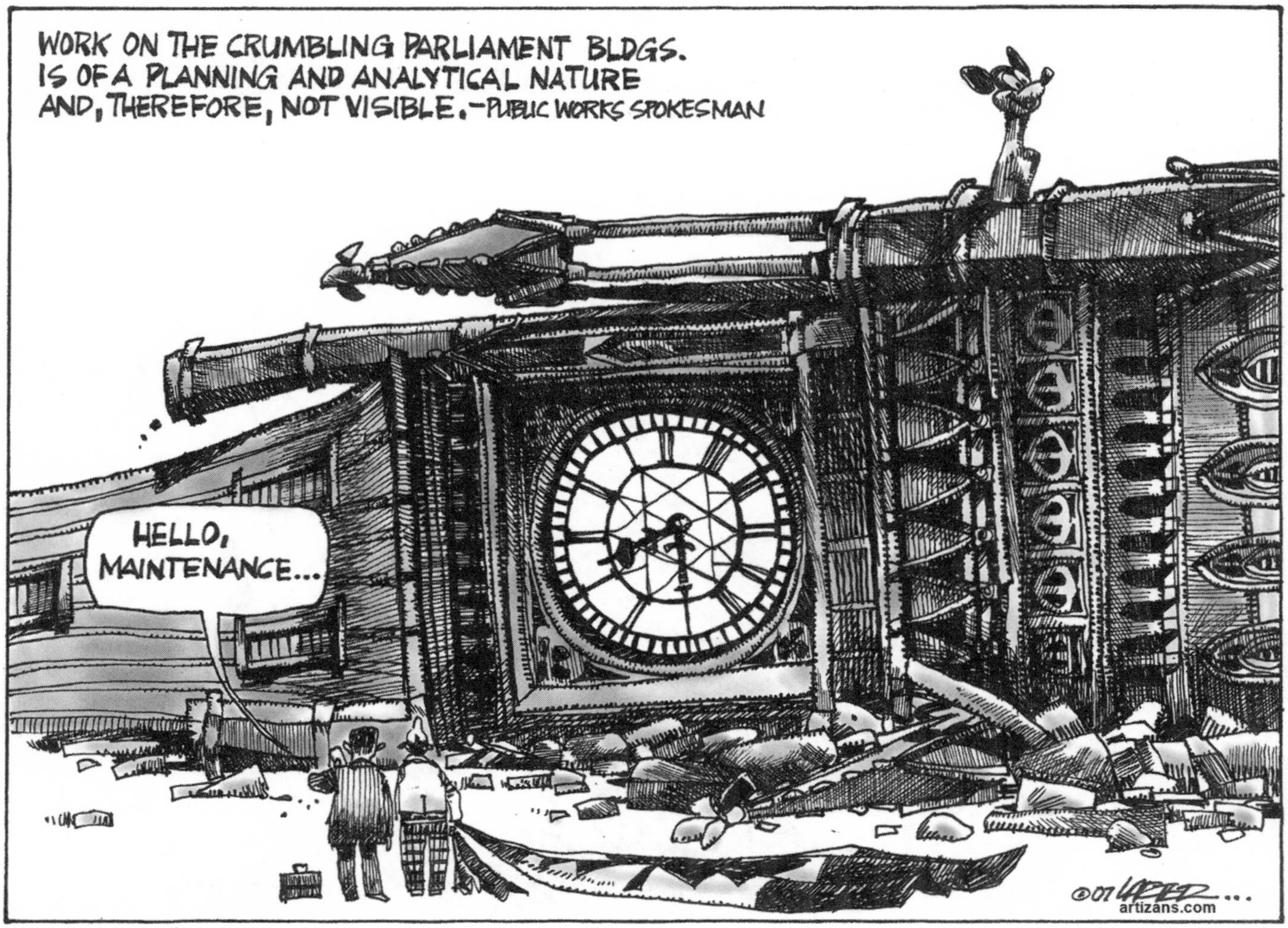
WORK ON THE CRUMBLING PARLIAMENT BLDGS. IS OF A PLANNING AND ANALYTICAL NATURE AND, THEREFORE, NOT VISIBLE. -PUBLIC WORKS SPOKESMAN
HELLO, MAINTENANCE...
©07 LARTER...
artizans.com

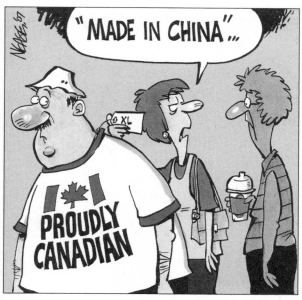

STEVE NEASE
Courtesy Toronto Sun

STEVE NEASE
Courtesy Toronto Sun

GRAEME MacKAY
Courtesy Hamilton Spectator

MALCOLM MAYES
Courtesy Edmonton Journal

JOHN LARTER
Courtesy Calgary Sun

# . . . and Other Issues

Queen Elizabeth visited the United States during the 400th anniversary of the English settlement of Jamestown.

Anna Nicole Smith, the blonde *Playboy* centerfold, reality-show subject, and widow of an octogenarian billionaire, died after collapsing in a Florida hotel. A court battle ensued among various individuals over who was to get custody of her baby and who was its father. Larry Birkhead, Smith's ex-boy friend, eventually was pronounced the father and granted custody.

Britain angered Muslims by knighting Salman Rushdie, who remained under death threats in Iran for allegedly insulting the prophet Mohammed in the book *The Satanic Verses*. It was revealed that wounded U.S. troops being cared for at Walter Reed Army Hospital were receiving substandard treatment. At first glance, the problem appeared scandalous, and a mad scramble ensued among the Pentagon, Congress, and the Army to fix it.

After years of criticism of the Guantanamo Bay detention center, the Bush Administration began formulating plans to close it.

ED GAMBLE
Courtesy Florida Times-Union

ED HALL
Courtesy Baker County Press

GARY VARVEL
Courtesy Indianapolis Star

JIM MORIN
Courtesy Miami Herald

CHRIS BRITT
Courtesy State Journal-Register (Ill.)

ADAM ZYGLIS
Courtesy Buffalo News

JOE HELLER
Courtesy Green Bay Press-Gazette

ROB ROGERS
Courtesy Pittsburgh Post-Gazette

ETTA HULME
Courtesy Fort Worth Star-Telegram

AARON TAYLOR
Courtesy Daily Herald (Utah)

DAVID HITCH
Courtesy Worcester Telegram & Gazette

MIKE PETERS
Courtesy Dayton Daily News

MALCOLM MAYES
Courtesy Edmonton Journal

DANA SUMMERS
Courtesy Orlando Sentinel

GRAEME MacKAY
Courtesy Hamilton Spectator

JIM BUSH
Courtesy Providence Journal (R.I.)

HAP PITKIN
Courtesy Boulder Camera

STEVE BREEN
Courtesy San Diego Union-Tribune

GUY BADEAUX
Courtesy LeDroit (Ottawa)

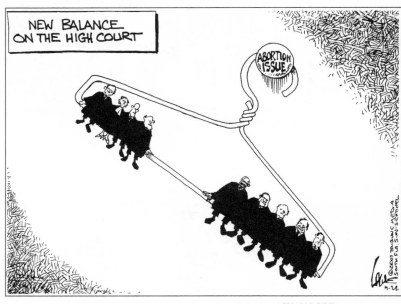

CHAN LOWE
Courtesy Fort Lauderdale News/
Sun Sentinel

JOE R. LANE
Courtesy Joe R. Lane

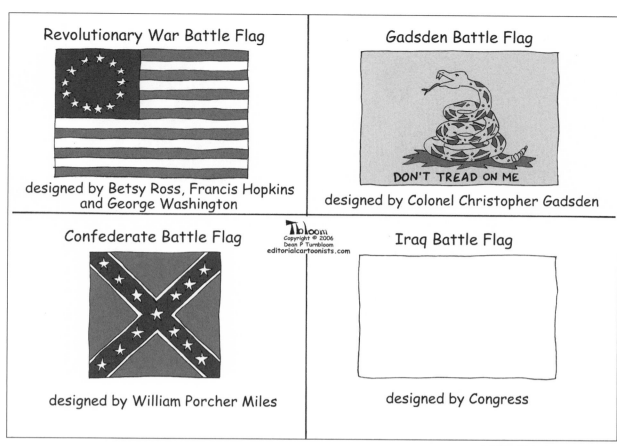

DEAN TURNBLOOM
Courtesy editorialcartoonists.com

ROB ROGERS
Courtesy Pittsburgh Post-Gazette

"WHAT HACKERS?"

DARREL AKERS
Courtesy The Reporter (Calif.)

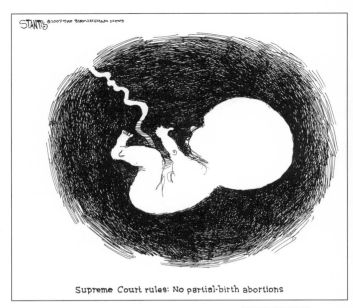

Supreme Court rules: No partial-birth abortions

SCOTT STANTIS
Courtesy Birmingham News

STEVE LINDSTROM
Courtesy Duluth News-Tribune

BOB LANG
Courtesy Editorial Services

JOHN RILEY
Courtesy rileycartoons.com

BOB ENGLEHART
Courtesy Hartford Courant

ETTA HULME
Courtesy Fort Worth Star-Telegram

JOE HOFFECKER
Courtesy Cincinnati Business Courier

JACK HIGGINS
Courtesy Chicago Sun-Times

CHARLIE HALL
Courtesy Rhode Island News Group

The President goes to Walter Reed Hospital to apologize in person.

197

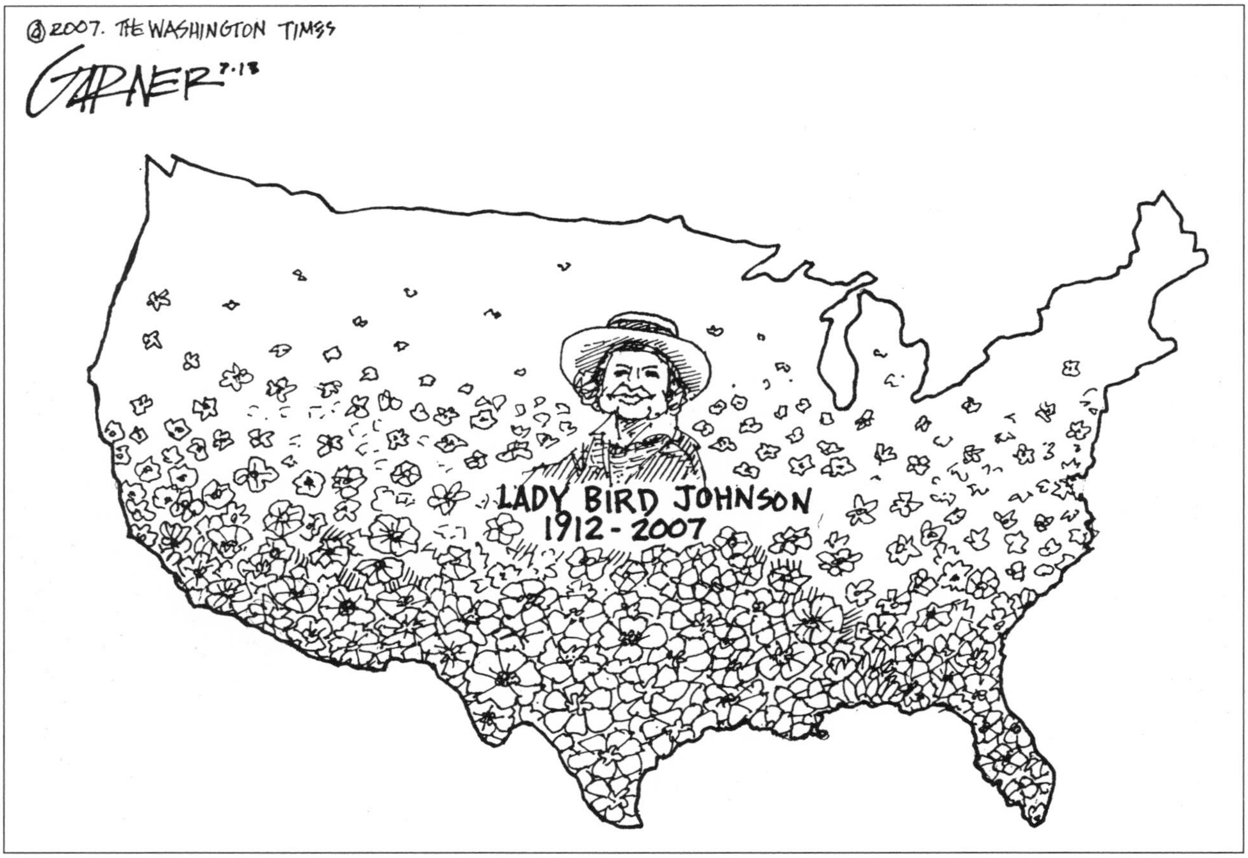
©2007. THE WASHINGTON TIMES
GARNER 7·18
LADY BIRD JOHNSON
1912 - 2007

BILL GARNER
Courtesy Washington Times

TOM STIGLICH
Courtesy Northeast Times (Pa.)

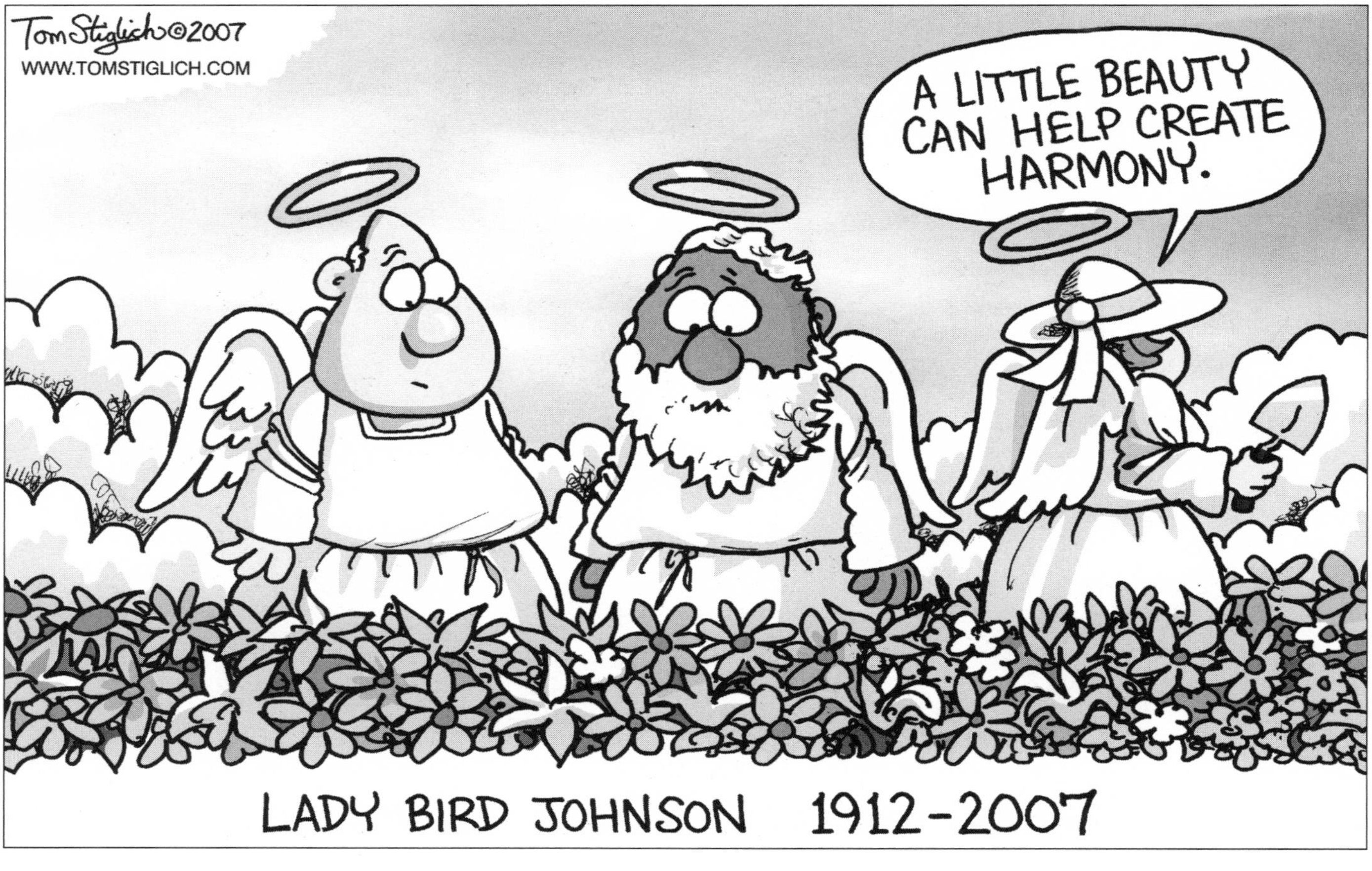
Tom Stiglich ©2007
WWW.TOMSTIGLICH.COM
A LITTLE BEAUTY CAN HELP CREATE HARMONY.
LADY BIRD JOHNSON 1912-2007

# In Memoriam

Cartoonists paid tribute to a number of notables who died during the year, including former President Gerald Ford, former first lady Lady Bird Johnson, opera singer Luciano Pavarotti, all-star New York Yankees shortstop and broadcaster Phil Rizzuto, former Soviet Union leader Boris Yeltsin, and creator of comic strips *B.C.* and *The Wizard of Id* Johnny Hart.

DOUG MacGREGOR
Courtesy Fort Myers News-Press

Luciano Pavarotti
1935 - 2007

JOHN R. ROSE
Courtesy Byrd Newspapers/
Daily News Record (Va.)

GARY MARKSTEIN
Courtesy Copley News Service

GEORGE DANBY
Courtesy Bangor Daily News

RANDY BISH
Courtesy Tribune-Review (Pa.)

201

S.C. RAWLS
Courtesy The Citizen

VIC HARVILLE
Courtesy Stephens Media Group

# Past Award Winners

## PULITZER PRIZE

1922—Rollin Kirby, New York World
1923—No award given
1924—J.N. Darling, New York Herald-Tribune
1925—Rollin Kirby, New York World
1926—D.R. Fitzpatrick, St. Louis Post-Dispatch
1927—Nelson Harding, Brooklyn Eagle
1928—Nelson Harding, Brooklyn Eagle
1929—Rollin Kirby, New York World
1930—Charles Macauley, Brooklyn Eagle
1931—Edmund Duffy, Baltimore Sun
1932—John T. McCutcheon, Chicago Tribune
1933—H.M. Talburt, Washington Daily News
1934—Edmund Duffy, Baltimore Sun
1935—Ross A. Lewis, Milwaukee Journal
1936—No award given
1937—C.D. Batchelor, New York Daily News
1938—Vaughn Shoemaker, Chicago Daily News
1939—Charles G. Werner, Daily Oklahoman
1940—Edmund Duffy, Baltimore Sun
1941—Jacob Burck, Chicago Times
1942—Herbert L. Block, NEA
1943—Jay N. Darling, New York Herald-Tribune
1944—Clifford K. Berryman, Washington Star
1945—Bill Mauldin, United Features Syndicate
1946—Bruce Russell, Los Angeles Times
1947—Vaughn Shoemaker, Chicago Daily News
1948—Reuben L. ("Rube") Goldberg, New York Sun
1949—Lute Pease, Newark Evening News
1950—James T. Berryman, Washington Star
1951—Reginald W. Manning, Arizona Republic
1952—Fred L. Packer, New York Mirror
1953—Edward D. Kuekes, Cleveland Plain Dealer
1954—Herbert L. Block, Washington Post
1955—Daniel R. Fitzpatrick, St. Louis Post-Dispatch
1956—Robert York, Louisville Times
1957—Tom Little, Nashville Tennessean
1958—Bruce M. Shanks, Buffalo Evening News
1959—Bill Mauldin, St. Louis Post-Dispatch
1960—No award given
1961—Carey Orr, Chicago Tribune
1962—Edmund S. Valtman, Hartford Times
1963—Frank Miller, Des Moines Register
1964—Paul Conrad, Denver Post
1965—No award given
1966—Don Wright, Miami News
1967—Patrick B. Oliphant, Denver Post
1968—Eugene Gray Payne, Charlotte Observer
1969—John Fischetti, Chicago Daily News
1970—Thomas F. Darcy, Newsday
1971—Paul Conrad, Los Angeles Times
1972—Jeffrey K. MacNelly, Richmond News Leader
1973—No award given
1974—Paul Szep, Boston Globe
1975—Garry Trudeau, Universal Press Syndicate

1976—Tony Auth, Philadelphia Enquirer
1977—Paul Szep, Boston Globe
1978—Jeff MacNelly, Richmond News Leader
1979—Herbert Block, Washington Post
1980—Don Wright, Miami News
1981—Mike Peters, Dayton Daily News
1982—Ben Sargent, Austin American-Statesman
1983—Dick Locher, Chicago Tribune
1984—Paul Conrad, Los Angeles Times
1985—Jeff MacNelly, Chicago Tribune
1986—Jules Feiffer, Universal Press Syndicate
1987—Berke Breathed, Washington Post Writers Group
1988—Doug Marlette, Atlanta Constitution
1989—Jack Higgins, Chicago Sun-Times
1990—Tom Toles, Buffalo News
1991—Jim Borgman, Cincinnati Enquirer
1992—Signe Wilkinson, Philadelphia Daily News
1993—Steve Benson, Arizona Republic
1994—Michael Ramirez, Memphis Commercial Appeal
1995—Mike Luckovich, Atlanta Constitution
1996—Jim Morin, Miami Herald
1997—Walt Handelsman, New Orleans Times-Picayune
1998—Steve Breen, Asbury Park Press
1999—David Horsey, Seattle Post-Intelligencer
2000—Joel Pett, Lexington Herald-Leader
2001—Ann Telnaes, Tribune Media Services
2002—Clay Bennett, Christian Science Monitor
2003—David Horsey, Seattle Post-Intelligencer
2004—Matt Davies, The Journal News
2005—Nick Anderson, Louisville Courier-Journal
2006—Mike Luckovich, Atlanta Journal-Constitution
2007—Walt Handelsman, Newsday

## SIGMA DELTA CHI AWARD

1942—Jacob Burck, Chicago Times
1943—Charles Werner, Chicago Sun
1944—Henry Barrow, Associated Press
1945—Reuben L. Goldberg, New York Sun
1946—Dorman H. Smith, NEA
1947—Bruce Russell, Los Angeles Times
1948—Herbert Block, Washington Post
1949—Herbert Block, Washington Post
1950—Bruce Russell, Los Angeles Times
1951—Herbert Block, Washington Post and
          Bruce Russell, Los Angeles Times
1952—Cecil Jensen, Chicago Daily News
1953—John Fischetti, NEA
1954—Calvin Alley, Memphis Commercial Appeal
1955—John Fischetti, NEA
1956—Herbert Block, Washington Post
1957—Scott Long, Minneapolis Tribune
1958—Clifford H. Baldowski, Atlanta Constitution
1959—Charles G. Brooks, Birmingham News
1960—Dan Dowling, New York Herald-Tribune

# PAST AWARD WINNERS

1961—Frank Interlandi, Des Moines Register
1962—Paul Conrad, Denver Post
1963—William Mauldin, Chicago Sun-Times
1964—Charles Bissell, Nashville Tennessean
1965—Roy Justus, Minneapolis Star
1966—Patrick Oliphant, Denver Post
1967—Eugene Payne, Charlotte Observer
1968—Paul Conrad, Los Angeles Times
1969—William Mauldin, Chicago Sun-Times
1970—Paul Conrad, Los Angeles Times
1971—Hugh Haynie, Louisville Courier-Journal
1972—William Mauldin, Chicago Sun-Times
1973—Paul Szep, Boston Globe
1974—Mike Peters, Dayton Daily News
1975—Tony Auth, Philadelphia Enquirer
1976—Paul Szep, Boston Globe
1977—Don Wright, Miami News
1978—Jim Borgman, Cincinnati Enquirer
1979—John P. Trever, Albuquerque Journal
1980—Paul Conrad, Los Angeles Times
1981—Paul Conrad, Los Angeles Times
1982—Dick Locher, Chicago Tribune
1983—Rob Lawlor, Philadelphia Daily News

1984—Mike Lane, Baltimore Evening Sun
1985—Doug Marlette, Charlotte Observer
1986—Mike Keefe, Denver Post
1987—Paul Conrad, Los Angeles Times
1988—Jack Higgins, Chicago Sun-Times
1989—Don Wright, Palm Beach Post
1990—Jeff MacNelly, Chicago Tribune
1991—Walt Handelsman, New Orleans Times-Picayune
1992—Robert Ariail, Columbia State
1993—Herbert Block, Washington Post
1994—Jim Borgman, Cincinnati Enquirer
1995—Michael Ramirez, Memphis Commercial Appeal
1996—Paul Conrad, Los Angeles Times
1997—Michael Ramirez, Los Angeles Times
1998—Jack Higgins, Chicago Sun-Times
1999—Mike Thompson, Detroit Free Press
2000—Nick Anderson, Louisville Courier-Journal
2001—Clay Bennett, Christian Science Monitor
2002—Mike Thompson, Detroit Free Press
2003—Steve Sack, Minneapolis Star-Tribune
2004—John Sherffius, jsherffius@aol.com
2005—Mike Luckovich, Atlanta Journal-Constitution
2006—Mike Lester, Rome News-Tribune

# Index of Cartoonists

# INDEX OF CARTOONISTS

# Complete Your CARTOON COLLECTION

Previous editions of this timeless classic are available for those wishing to update their collection of the most provocative moments of the past three decades. Most important, in the end, the wit and wisdom of the editorial cartoonists prevail on the pages of these op-ed editorials, where one can find memories and much, much more in the work of the nation's finest cartoonists.

## Select from the following supply of past editions

| | | |
|---|---|---|
| _____ 1972 Edition $20.00 pb (F) | _____ 1986 Edition $20.00 pb (F) | _____ 1999 Edition $20.00 pb |
| _____ 1974 Edition $20.00 pb (F) | _____ 1987 Edition $20.00 pb | _____ 2000 Edition $20.00 pb |
| _____ 1975 Edition $20.00 pb (F) | _____ 1988 Edition $20.00 pb | _____ 2001 Edition $20.00 pb |
| _____ 1976 Edition $20.00 pb (F) | _____ 1989 Edition $20.00 pb (F) | _____ 2002 Edition $14.95 pb |
| _____ 1977 Edition $20.00 pb (F) | _____ 1990 Edition $20.00 pb | _____ 2003 Edition $14.95 pb |
| _____ 1978 Edition $20.00 pb (F) | _____ 1991 Edition $20.00 pb | _____ 2004 Edition $14.95 pb |
| _____ 1979 Edition $20.00 pb (F) | _____ 1992 Edition $20.00 pb | _____ 2005 Edition $14.95 pb |
| _____ 1980 Edition $20.00 pb (F) | _____ 1993 Edition $20.00 pb | _____ 2006 Edition $14.95 pb |
| _____ 1981 Edition $20.00 pb (F) | _____ 1994 Edition $20.00 pb | _____ 2007 Edition $14.95 pb |
| _____ 1982 Edition $20.00 pb (F) | _____ 1995 Edition $20.00 pb | _____ 2008 Edition $14.95 pb |
| _____ 1983 Edition $20.00 pb (F) | _____ 1996 Edition $20.00 pb | |
| _____ 1984 Edition $20.00 pb (F) | _____ 1997 Edition $20.00 pb | _____ Add me to the list of standing orders |
| _____ 1985 Edition $20.00 pb (F) | _____ 1998 Edition $20.00 pb | |

Please include $2.95 for 4th Class Postage and handling or $6.85 for UPS Ground Shipment plus $.75 for each additional copy ordered.

Total enclosed: _____

NAME _____

ADDRESS _____

CITY_____ STATE_____ ZIP_____

Make checks payable to:

**PELICAN PUBLISHING COMPANY**
1000 Burmaster St., Dept. 6BEC
Gretna, Louisiana 70053-2246

**CREDIT CARD ORDERS CALL 1-800-843-1724 or or go to e-pelican.com/store**
Jefferson Parish residents add 8¾% tax. All other Louisiana residents add 4% tax.
Please visit our Web site at www.pelicanpub.com or e-mail us at sales@pelicanpub.com